Conversations
with a One Year Old

Conversations
with a One Year Old

A Case Study of the
Developmental Foundation of Syntax

RONALD SCOLLON

The University Press of Hawaii
and
The Research Corporation of the University of Hawaii
Honolulu

Manufactured in the United States of America.
Composition by Asco Trade Typesetting Ltd., Hong Kong

Library of Congress Cataloging in Publication Data

Scollon, Ronald, 1939–
    Conversations with a one year old.

    Bibliography: p.
    1. Children—Language. 2. Child psychology.
I. Title. [DNLM: 1. Linguistics. 2. Language
Development. 3. Psycholinguistics. LB1139.L3 S422c]
P118.S3   401′.9   76–24881
ISBN 0–8248–0479–1

tape
tape
    word
    word
    word
    word
    word
        paper
        paper
        paper
        paper
        paper
            pen
            pen
                tape
                tape

                    BRENDA WONG

Contents

Tables

Preface

This book is a distillation of many happy afternoons my wife and I spent with Brenda Wong, her sister Charlotte, and the mother of these two children. As with all distillations, as purity is gained some of the original flavor is lost. In the following pages these happy afternoons have been distilled into the "taping sessions" or "recording sessions" of a case study. Here I want to express my gratitude to these participants for making these visits always a pleasure. To Brenda, who will soon be able to read this, and to Charlotte, who can now read it I want to say thank you for helping me to make this book.

This study began as a project for a seminar on language acquisition, grew to a PhD dissertation, and has now been recast as a book. In the process I have incurred a considerable debt of gratitude to the people who have guided me in this research. Dr. Michael L. Forman, as the teacher of the original seminar, and as my mentor has never failed to achieve the best balance between personal encouragement and incisive criticism. Dr. Ann Marie Peters, Dr. Donald M. Topping, and Dr. Robert Hsu have all read the manuscript and offered valuable insights as well as reminded me that I have still not perfectly acquired my language. I also want to thank Dr. Robert Hsu for helping me with the computer programs. Mr. Geoffrey Nathan, who was asked to read the manuscript under the pressure of an examination, suggested valuable additions.

During the spring of 1973 an informal seminar met in the linguistics department of the University of Hawaii in which many of my ideas were critically discussed. The present form of these ideas was importantly molded in those discussions. I wish to thank all the participants, but particularly Dr. Gregory Lee and Dr. Paul Kay for their questions and suggestions about my work. Although he did not regularly attend those sessions, Dr. David Reibel also suggested valuable lines of thought.

My wife, Suzanne, has been actively involved in every aspect of this study and I find it difficult to express the extent of my gratitude to her.

In acknowledging the contributions of others to this study I do not want to implicate them in its conclusions. In some cases the most helpful contribution has been disagreement. Undoubtedly many of the conclusions that are presented in the following pages will have to be changed or discarded in the light of future research in language development. If the descriptive aspects of this presentation have been made clear enough to be of use to future investigators its purpose will be served.

SECTION I

Organization

CHAPTER I

Introduction

I.1 Vertical Construction

At age one year, seven months and two days the little girl in this study picked up her mother's shoe, held it right before her eyes and while she stared at it said, [mama . mama . mama . mam . š . ši . šiš . šu . šu ʔ . šuš]. (Appendix A explains the symbols used.) I think that what she said is understandable as 'mama's shoe'. I think that it was intentional, and that the utterance expresses a semantic relation that is not expressed by either word. This relation is expressed by means of a construction. Further, the whole expresses a single speech act, a predication. I have called constructions of this type "vertical constructions," and they are the structural focal point of this study.

Studies of child language have dealt with sentences. In this study I have called sentences "horizontal constructions" to distinguish them from vertical constructions. The difference between them, in a few words, is that horizontal constructions (sentences) express constructional relations under a single utterance intonation contour. In vertical constructions the utterance contour is applied to each part of the construction.

I argue for the importance of vertical construction on the grounds that these constructions are the developmental basis for horizontal constructions. In addition, once horizontal constructions are developed, vertical construction continues as an active process, resulting in more complex constructions.

In making my argument for vertical constructions, I point out that they develop for the child in interaction with other speakers on the one hand and repetition of the child's own utterances on the other. I further argue that this mechanism of interaction and repetition is not specific to syntactic development but is general to language development. I suggest that this process follows on earlier nonlinguistic sensorimotor developments.

I.2   Vertical Construction and Linguistic Method

The question then arises: If vertical construction is such an important process of language acquisition why have other investigators not been concerned with it? The answer has to do with the method of research. In some cases the focus on a specific aspect of development such as the sentence or phonology has prevented investigators from seeing the interplay between these separate aspects. In most cases, a focus that has been too narrow has explicitly excluded from study three types of data on which this study is crucially founded—one-word utterances, repetitions, and unintelligible utterances. Since the first vertical constructions are sequences of single-word utterances, the exclusion of these from study effectively eliminates vertical constructions from consideration. In the study of the development of repetition, I found that I could show that vertical construction progresses from initially highly tentative constructions that are largely dependent on interaction with other speakers to constructions in which the child shows a large measure of control and independence. Finally, the inclusion of unintelligible utterances was important because many of these could be understood by an increased use of the context of the situation and my own developing knowledge of the child's system. I found that some of these unintelligible utterances were, in fact, unintelligible because of their presence in constructions.

This methodological issue is the main point of this study. By narrowing the focus to some specific aspect of language acquisition before undertaking the study, other investigators have effectively excluded the data that are needed to understand vertical construction and, ultimately, horizontal construction as well. In this study, I have taken a broader focus and in doing so have found that horizontal constructions (sentences) are a later development which is begun in vertical construction. I argue that this developmental process can only be seen when a more holistic focus is taken. This holistic focus must include discourse and functional structuring as well as the more traditional aspects of phonology and syntax.

I.3   Organization of this Study

This presentation is organized with nine chapters divided into three sections, plus appendices and bibliography. The first section deals with the organization of the study. This first chapter introduces the presentation. The second chapter describes in detail how the primary data of this study were collected and studied. In the interest of comparability, I have given considerable detail. One of the difficulties in dealing with studies of child language is that many of them simply cannot be compared with other studies because of a lack of information about the data. Chapter two is intended to make the data of this study as fully comparable as possible. In general, I have followed Brown (1973) in details of notation. I have specifically tried to make clear what data have been included or excluded at the level of recording, transcription, analysis, and, finally, at the level of presentation.

The second section consists of four chapters in which I present everything but construction. Chapter three discusses phonology from a quite early stage up to the beginning of horizontal (sentence) construction. In the study of phonology some questions are first raised. For example, I have discussed (1) the treatment of repetition, (2) my understanding of imitation, (3) the means of arriving at glosses for the child's utterances, and (4) the interaction of phonology and construction.

Chapter four is a study of the development of intonation. Sentences have been defined in the literature by reference to primary stress and terminal intonation contour. In this study, I show that this intonation develops during the early one-word period and that it continues to interact with subsequent phonological developments until it reaches a condition of relative stability just before the beginning of horizontal construction.

Chapter five deals with what I call discourse redundancies. These are imitation and repetition. Imitation repeats (is redundant in relation to) another speaker. Repetition repeats (is redundant in relation to) the same speaker—in this case the child. These two processes work to expand the child's system. Imitation provides models for advancement while repetition practices variation within the current system. Both processes first work in development of phonology and then later in the development of syntax.

Chapter six is about discourse itself. Very early in this study I noticed that the child 'talked' with other speakers. Discourse is the interactive space of the child's communication with the mature language. I found that vertical constructions develop out of these interactions. That is, the child's system develops in interactions with the adult system. On the other hand, the adult system undergoes quite striking changes in interactions with children. These changes are more extreme in the early stages and less extreme as the child develops. It appears that the adult extends his system as fully as possible at first to maximize the communication overlap and then gradually withdraws the extension and in the process leads the child toward the mature system.

The third section is directly about construction. Chapter seven discusses the constructions I have found from an external point of view. Vertical constructions are shown to exist in at least four types that are cross classified on the dimensions of repetitions and discourse. I show that vertical constructions with many repetitions precede in development vertical constructions with fewer and finally no repetitions of the elements in construction. At the same time, the need for interaction with other speakers to produce constructions declines with time. These two developments converge on a type of vertical construction that is distinguishable from horizontal construction only by intonation pattern and the presence of a pause between the elements. I also show that these same four types are present in the following period of horizontal construction.

Chapter eight discusses the internal structure of horizontal constructions and vertical constructions, First, I approach these constructions from the point of view of orderings of word classes. Then, I consider constructions from the point of view of the expression of semantic relations.

Chapter nine places horizontal construction and vertical construction in the context of function. In the earliest period, there is a close correspondence between form and function, but, by the end of the second year of life, form and function have been separated into a complex system. Finally, I review the way in which I have observed separate aspects of development to interact.

It should be apparent that there is a considerable amount of restatement throughout this presentation. This is caused by the general problem of exegesis that in order to understand one of two points one must be familiar with the other one. Since it is not possible to place both points first, I have adopted the means of rather frequent recapitulation. Since the focal point is vertical construction and the methodology that led to this study of vertical construction, this discussion had to be placed later in the presentation where it could be seen to be based on a foundation of the earlier discussions of phonology, intonation, and discourse. The reader would be able to get a reasonable understanding of my main points by reading only Section III. For support of any of the conclusions of that section, however, the reader will need to refer to the earlier discussion in Section II.

CHAPTER II

The Data

II.1 Elements of the Recording Sessions

This section will discuss the three main elements of the recording sessions: The subjects, the setting, and the recording equipment.

II.1.1 The Subjects

The primary subject of this study is Brenda Wong. I have not chosen a pseudonym for her for two reasons. Her first name appears so frequently in the data that the use of a pseudonym would introduce the problem of alteration of the raw data itself. This would be particularly problematic in the area of phonology. The second reason is that Brenda's last name, Wong, is found at a high enough frequency in Honolulu that her anonymity is effectively safeguarded.

At the beginning of this study Brenda was one year and two days old (1;0.2). (In the interest of comparability, I am following the age notation of Brown [1973].) At the last session she was two years and twelve days old (2;0.12). Brenda is a normal, healthy child. When she was quite young, her parents had her tested by an audiologist because they suspected some hearing deficiency. The audiologist also suspected a hearing deficiency but recommended waiting to watch her early speech development for confirmation.

Brenda's development during the time of this study both in her speech and in general has allayed any fears her parents might have once had. Her talkativeness and willingness to participate, not to mention her sense of humor, have facilitated the study of her speech.

Brenda is the second child in her family. Her older sister, Charlotte, was four years and six days old (4;0.6) at the beginning of this study. Charlotte was present in all of the recording sessions except one and as a result is often very actively participating. I did not try to exclude Charlotte from the recording, but my focus on Brenda sometimes precipitated competition between the two sisters. On the whole, Charlotte learned to take a secondary role during the time of the recordings and finally began to try to prompt Brenda's speech for show.

In the course of the year covered by this study, Charlotte taught herself to read. Her parents have made no specific attempts to teach her, but there is a general environment of reading in the home. As a result of the mother's reading to them and also probably of Charlotte's reading as well, Brenda has developed much interest in books. These are the only two children in the home.

The parents of these children are in their early thirties. The father is Chinese, born in Hawaii. His speech is best called Hawaiian English or Creole. He has a college education and is a partner in an accounting firm. He was present only in three of the early recording sessions so his speech is not directly involved to any great extent as data. However, Brenda sees a lot of her father. Since the children play together with him for several hours each evening, he can certainly be considered an important influence in their development. Although the father was raised by parents who were bilingual in English and Chinese, his use of Chinese is quite limited.

The mother was born in Japan and moved to Hawaii with her family when she was about twelve. She went to college for several years but did not finish a degree. The mother speaks Japanese as her first language but also speaks Standard English in variation with what might be called Japanese Hawaiian English. She is not employed, and spends most of her time in the home with the children. The mother was present in all of the recording sessions, and her speech in interaction with Brenda is an important part of this work.

My wife, Suzanne, and I were the two participant-observers

in this study. I had originally thought that our participation would be minimal and that we would record mostly mother-child interactions. As the study progressed, however, my interactions with Brenda became more central, and only Suzanne remained in the position of an observer. Our relationship with the family was established before the study. Brenda's father is Suzanne's uncle. Suzanne was born in Hawaii and first learned Hawaiian English and some Cantonese. Later, she learned Standard English. Her speech now is best characterized as varying between Standard and Hawaiian English.

My own part in this study became quite central. As Brenda and I got to know each other, our interactions became quite fluent. At the same time, the other subjects tended to retire to the background whenever they knew that I was there for business. Without trying to do anything more than focus the microphone on Brenda for the time of the recording, I apparently claimed more or less exclusive rights to her attention during the time of the recordings. For the first eighteen years of my life, I spoke only Standard English (Midwestern). In some cases of imitation, it is my speech being imitated. To what extent my speech has had any lasting effect on Brenda's development is hard to say. Her speech and apparently her mother's speech have had an effect on my speech at least during the recording sessions. (See VI.6 on adult speech.)

Table 1 lists the recording sessions in considerable detail. The subjects above are abbreviated as follows: Brenda, B; Charlotte, Ch; Mother, M; Father, F; Ron, R; Suzanne, S. In one session (042—see II.2.2.6 for discussion of this notation) a neighbor named Jill (eight years of age) was present. In one other session (151–152) many others were present. That tape has not been considered of central importance to this study. On the whole, Brenda, Charlotte, the mother, Suzanne and I were the participants in all of the tapes. Further detail on the characteristics of adult speech are given where directly relevant to the discussion.

II.1.2   The Setting

All of the recordings except two were made in Brenda's home in Honolulu. In the first several sessions, before she learned to walk, I recorded her mostly in the same place in the living room. When

TABLE 1. Summary of the Tapes

Tape	Date	Age	Time	Place	People Present
BRENDA I					
011	Feb. 12, 1972	1;0.2	11:00 a.m.	Brenda's	Ch, M, R, S
012	Feb. 12, 1972	1;0.2	11:30 a.m.	home	B, Ch, M, R, S
021	Feb. 19, 1972	1;0.9	12:15 p.m.	"	B, Ch, M, R, S
022	Feb. 26, 1972	1;0.16	8:55 a.m.	"	B, Ch, M, F, R, S
031	Mar. 4, 1972	1;0.23	8:50 a.m.	"	B, Ch, M, F, R, S
032	Mar. 12, 1972	1;1.2	9:45 a.m.	"	B, Ch, M, R, S
041	Mar. 18, 1972	1;1.8	10:45 a.m.	"	B, M, R, S
042	Mar. 25, 1972	1;1.15	9:50 a.m.	"	B, Ch, Jill, M, R, S
051	Apr. 1, 1972	1;1.22	10:45 a.m.	"	B, Ch, M, R, S
052	Apr. 9, 1972	1;1.29	10:30 a.m.	"	B, Ch, M, R, S
ET1[a]	Apr. 9, 1972	1;1.29	11:00 a.m.	"	B, Ch, M, R, S
061	Apr. 15, 1972	1;2.5	10:45 a.m.	R's apt.	B, Ch, M, R, S
S11[b]	Apr. 29, 1972	1;2.19	?	R's apt.	B, Ch, M, R, S

BRENDA II

071, 072	Sep. 12, 1972	1;7.2	1:40 p.m.	Brenda's	B, Ch, M, R, S
081, 082	Sep. 19, 1972	1;7.9	2:00 p.m.	home	B, Ch, M, R, S
091, 092	Sep. 26, 1972	1;7.16	12:30 p.m.	"	B, Ch, M, R, S
101, 102	Oct. 3, 1972	1;7.23	4:20 p.m.	"	B, Ch, M, R, S
111, 112	Oct. 10, 1972	1;8	12:00 noon	"	B, Ch, M, R, S
121, 122	Oct. 17, 1972	1;8.7	3:00 p.m.	"	B, Ch, M, R, S
131, 132	Oct. 24, 1972	1;8.14	2:00 p.m.	"	B, Ch, M, R, S
141, 142	Oct. 31, 1972	1;8.21	3:00 p.m.	"	B, Ch, M, R, S

BRENDA III

151, 152	Dec. 23, 1972	1;10.13	7:00 p.m.	"	B, Ch, F, M, R, S, and many others
161, 162	Dec. 27, 1972	1;10.17	2:00 p.m.	"	B, Ch, M, R, S

BRENDA IV

171, 172	Feb. 22, 1973	2;0.12	3:00 p.m.	"	B, Ch, M, R, S

[a] Experimental Tape 1 (ET1) was made to record a session immediately following (052) in which I tried to elicit specific words with photographs.
[b] Summer 1 Side 1 (S11) was made two weeks after the session called (061) as a follow-up but has not entered significantly into this study.

she started getting around and learned that I would follow, she began a game (of which she is still not tired) seeing how far and fast she can pull me along behind her. As a result, the recordings have been taken in most parts of the house and outdoors in the yard.

The house has three bedrooms (each child has her own) and a large living room-dining area. There is also a large enclosed patio. It is furnished in a style common in Hawaii that mixes Japanese and Western elements. All footwear is left outside and inside there are both chairs for Western-style seating and cushions for sitting on the floor. For these sessions, we were rarely anywhere but on the floor when we were inside. Outside in the yard are a sandbox and a swing-slide set.

Since my wife and I are related to Brenda and her family, we sometimes see them at times other than the scheduled sessions. This has afforded a chance to make an informal comparison of our interactions in different settings. Although the sessions recorded for study were quite regular in both place and the people present, they were not at all uncharacteristic. The main difference was in the continuous attention Brenda received during the recordings. Brenda normally gets a lot of attention, but it is unlikely that she gets such predictably good attention from anyone else.

II.1.3   The Equipment

The tape recorder used was a Sony TC-110A with an F-26S microphone. At first it was used plugged in, but, later, as Brenda became more active, a Sony BP-9 Battery Pack was used for electrical power. Suzanne used a small notebook to make notes about the nonlinguistic context. This notebook often was used by Brenda for scribblings that she claimed were "nice." I made no attempt to conceal the tape recorder or the microphone, but I tried to avoid drawing any particular attention to it. The surprising depth of such a young child's understanding was demonstrated one time when she was 1;3.4. (This tape was not included in the main body of data because of an unusually large number of interruptions.) I had set up the tape recorder and Brenda took the microphone and held it up for different people to talk into it. Apparently in the twelve preceding sessions she had learned quite well what it was for.

On tape (111) Brenda demonstrated her understanding of our equipment and our roles. We were ignoring our things while we ate some ice cream. Brenda said, "tape, tape," then held the microphone up to Suzanne's mouth and said, "word, word, word, word, word." She then got the notebook and, as she handed it to Suzanne, said, "paper, paper, paper, paper, paper" then "pen, pen." She then picked up the whole tape recorder and gave it to me and said, "tape, tape."

I feel it would be a serious mistake to underestimate Brenda's awareness of the presence of our little equipment and its purpose. The family does not own a tape recorder of any kind, and the mother says that Brenda only knows about them from the one we brought. What is more, except for the first time we recorded, we haven't played recordings for the children and in that first session Brenda was asleep when we played back the tape for Charlotte. Brenda, then, couldn't have any any direct knowledge that the tape recorder could make any noises at all, let alone words. She did know, however, that its function had to do with saying words into it. This is in contrast to Bloom's (1970, p. 16) claim that "the children accepted the presence of the recording equipment as a natural extension of the investigator and they were unaware of its purpose."

II.1.4 Summary

This study looks at the interaction between a primary subject, Brenda Wong, and four secondary subjects, Charlotte, the mother, and my wife Suzanne and me. These interactions take place in Brenda's home and are recorded on a casette tape recorder while handwritten notes are taken to supplement the tapes with non-linguistic contextual information.

II.2 First-Level Selection

Since at the beginning this work was largely exploratory, I had few theoretical preconceptions to influence decisions about selecting data for study. Decisions about what to record and when, what to transcribe and how to encode the data for further manipulation were mostly made on the basis of convenience, and simply evolved with time. What follows is a detailed discussion of the mechanics of the collection and sorting of the data.

II.2.1 The Recordings

The first tape made was a full hour (two sides of a C-60 cassette). It was begun while Brenda was not present. I recorded the first half hour without her so that I would have a segment of tape on which she was not a participant. Since I had made no previous decisions about what I would consider relevant to my study, I taped a continuous hour thinking that later unimportant sections could be edited out. As the taping progressed over several weeks it became clear that many things considered irrelevant on first analysis became important for other reasons later. For this reason, a regular program of always taking a full thirty-minute tape without interruptions seemed preferable to stopping the tape and starting it. This, of course, relieved me of having to make any decisions at the time of taping about the relevance of any segment of interaction.

When the study was begun, it was impossible to find time to record any more frequently than once a week. This, then, was the pattern which became established. A continous thirty-minute recording was taken once a week on the same day of the week and as near as possible to the same time of day. For the first group of recordings (BRENDA I) this was on Saturday just after Brenda's morning nap. For the second group of recordings (BRENDA II), Tuesday afternoon was chosen. These decisions were based on my class schedule.

BRENDA I consists of a sequence of recordings taken in ten consecutive weeks starting at age 1;0.2 and ending at age 1;2.5. One further recording was made two weeks later. In the discussions that follow, the first eight sessions of this group of recordings are referred to as BRENDA I. I began this group of recordings as an exploratory study with the intention of looking at the development of intonation during the one-word period. As a result of course papers and examinations and then three months of field work in Alaska (which was unrelated to this study), it was five months before I was able to return to study Brenda. The second group of recordings (BRENDA II) was made starting five months after BRENDA I when Brenda was 1;7.2 and covered eight consecutive weeks up until age 1;8.21. BRENDA III (age 1;10.17) consists of two recordings taken two months after BRENDA II as a follow-up. Another single recording taken again two months after that is BRENDA IV (age 2;0.12).

The two main bodies of data, then, are BRENDA I and BRENDA II, with the few tapes of BRENDA III and IV added as a follow-up. This follow-up is continuing but is not taken to be a directly relevant part of this report. The details of these recording sessions are given in Table 1.

II.2.2 The Transcriptions

The pragmatics of transcription had much to do with the decision to limit the recordings to one half hour each week. Since no decision had been made about what would be relevant to the study, it seemed best to make a rather complete transcription of each tape. All of Brenda's utterances as well as those of all of the other speakers on the tape regardless of whether they were speaking directly to Brenda were transcribed. The amount of time involved in making these transcriptions made it impossible to do any more. I considered it very important to make all of the transcriptions within, at the most, several days of when the tape was taken. In working with the language of such a young child, the context of any utterance is crucial to determining both meaning and appropriateness and much of the contextual transcription depended on my memory of the situation. In addition to contextual information, a certain amount of "getting into" the transcription for any tape made the task easier. I felt that if I waited beyond any new recordings for a transcription I would run the risk of extrapolating later forms into earlier, less developed forms.

II.2.2.1 Technique of Transcription

The tapes were transcribed using the Sony TC110A and a Sony DR-7A Headphone adapted with cassette recorder miniplug. The headset considerably improved the phonetic detail and audibility. The transcriptions were written out on the back of discarded computer print-out paper which was wide enough to allow six columns (vertical), one for each speaker and one for notes on the nonlinguistic context. The transcription for Brenda was in phonetic notation. Her intonation was also transcribed. For other speakers, an orthographic transcription was used. This initial transcription was made in one session usually—in most cases the same day as the recording.

II.2.2.2 Phonetic Transcription of Brenda's Utterances

In making these transcriptions I felt increasingly dissatisfied with the set of symbols I was using. I felt, as Drachman (1973) has expressed, that the standard phonetic symbols developed for adult speech were simply inadequate for a narrow transcription of child speech. The symbols I used were largely those of the International Phonetic Alphabet but with a number of diacritic symbols added of my own invention. For example, a symbol was needed to indicate an ingressive airstream in several cases. Since making these transcriptions a working paper of the Stanford Child Language Project (Bush et al. 1973) has come to my attention in which a very useful set of diacritics for use in conjunction with IPA symbols for transcription of child speech has been developed. Although there are some differences between the symbols they have developed and the ones I have used, on the whole it is clear that the Stanford group has been encountering the same phonetic difficulties.

The particular areas in which a narrow transcription was difficult were in the intervocalic consonants and in the initial consonants where voicing was a consideration. A characteristic of the intervocalic consonants that was difficult to transcribe was a lack of constancy. Intervocalic consonants often sound like a series of transitions from vowel to vowel with the closure and amount of frication varying too quickly to be easily assigned any one symbol. On the other hand, the initial consonants shift freely between voicing and aspiration. If one symbol is taken to represent a voiced consonant, e.g. [d], another to represent a voiceless consonant, e.g. [t], and a third to represent an aspirated consonant, e.g. [tʰ], it is often difficult to assign any one of these to a particular segment. Both of these problems seem to be the result of the same process—that is, incomplete control of the vocal apparatus. The work begun by the Stanford group points the direction for essential research into this area of child phonetics.

II.2.2.3 Intonation Transcription of Brenda's Utterances

When I began transcribing, I had an interest in watching the development of stress and intonation, thinking they later might have importance in making syntactic distinctions in early construction as had been reported by Miller and Ervin (1964). Having had some years of background in musical dictation, my first approach to transcription of intonation was a musical notation. Since I had no idea what might become significant, I transcribed in detail on a music staff the exact pitches and relative rhythmic patterns using standard musical notation. By making a copy of the tape at $7\frac{1}{2}$ inches per second and then slowing it to half speed the utterance was lowered by one octave and played at half the speed. It was then fairly easy to transcribe the pitches with a considerable degree of confidence.

This type of notation was used for the first five tapes. It was later abandoned when a group of patterns was evident. Those patterns allowed a simpler set of symbols to be used. Since at the same time the number of utterances on each tape was rapidly increasing, there was the added pressure of the time it took to transcribe each tape phonetically. The chapter on intonation (IV.1.1) will discuss these intonation symbols in detail.

II.2.2.4 Contextual Transcription

During the recording sessions, Suzanne kept notes of the nonverbal and inaudible context. Naturally, the amount that can be written into notes is very limited, and there is the second problem of synchronizing the notes with the tape in making later transcriptions. For each note, Suzanne recorded the number on the tape meter. I found that it was very easy to learn to make spoken notes directly onto the tape at the time, and this greatly reduced the need of other notes. Throughout this study, particularly in this area of understanding the nonverbal context of an utterance, the need for videotaping was felt, but the cost was prohibitive.

II.2.2.5 Orthographic Transcription

All of the speakers other than Brenda were transcribed in a modified English orthography. In BRENDA III and IV Brenda's utterances were also transcribed orthographically. Certain substitutions for standard orthography were made when I felt that it was important to mark a difference in formality or style. For example, *gonna* replaced 'going to', *dis* and *dat* replaced 'this' and 'that'. A phonetic transcription was made in a few cases where the utterance was unintelligible but audible or where there was some unusual pronunciation that would be missed in the orthographic transcription. These orthographic transcriptions of Brenda's speech might better be called "orthographic translations" since what they preserve is meaning and word order. Phonetic shape is lost. In general, it seemed best to regard the transcription of other speakers as a guide through the interaction, and an exact phonetic transcription would not only take a lot of time to write but would be cumbersome to read.

II.2.2.6   Other Encoding of the Transcription

The tapes are numbered consecutively (1 through 17). Side one and side two of each tape is indicated by a 1 or a 2 after the tape number. For example, (101) represents tape ten side one, or (071) represents tape seven side one. As can be seen in Table 1 for the recordings of BRENDA I, each tape was used for two weeks. Starting with (071) a full hour was recorded each week with only the first side taken for data in this study. Side two was held in reserve in case it was felt that further information was desired for any particular week. The tapes of BRENDA III and IV were fully transcribed for both sides to increase the amount of data for each session since there was a two-month break between sessions.

Each utterance on each tape transcribed was numbered. In most cases, this raised no particular problems since the utterances were clearly isolated from each other in the early stages. By BRENDA III it became a real theoretical problem which will be taken up in this chapter, section three (II.3). Whatever the status of the utterance under any particular number, the number indicates its relative position on the tape. References to specific utterances, then, will be made by tape number and utterance number. For example (051)137 indicates the 137th utterance on the first side of tape five.

A further type of encoding developed somewhat by accident. The first transcription was written out in black ink. The context was written in with green ink to make it easier to separate from the voice transcription. The utterance numbers were written in red ink. In that case it was to keep from confusing the phonetic transcription and its diacritics with the numbers on an increasingly crowded transcription. The footage markers were noted in spaces of five feet in the left margin. The phonetic transcription, then, was made in a first listening. The utterance numbers and footage markers were made in a second listening. The intonation transcription was made in a third hearing. It often turned out that differences were noted in blue ink to separate them clearly from the original transcription. In this way it could be seen at a colorful glance to what extent the initial transcription of a particular utterance had withstood the minimum of three hearings. Table 2 gives a facsimile page of transcription.

II.2.2.7 Further Data Sorting

The next step was to get the data into a form that could be sorted using a computer. After making the transcriptions as described, all of Brenda's utterances for tapes (012) through (061)— BRENDA I—and tapes (071) through (141)—BRENDA II—were keypunched indicating tape number, utterance number, phonetic transcription, and intonation symbol. For BRENDA II a "gloss" was added for each utterance, i.e., an English adult translation of what Brenda said. These "glosses" will be discussed in more detail in several other sections. This information on the data card allowed a simple program to sort Brenda's utterances by chronological order, by intonation type, by phonetic form, and for BRENDA II by "gloss" or word that was understood by adults. Print-outs made on the basis of these sorts formed the data for all of the context-free parts of this study. Incidentally, it should be mentioned that it was in working with these same context-free print-outs that I began to experience frustration with the skeletal and unrealistic appearance of the data. Context-free print-outs eventually proved to be useless for anything but the most superficial studies of phonology and intonation.

One final type of sorting was to calculate the mean length of utterance for some of the sessions. Brown (1973) has argued for the use of the mean length of utterance (MLU) as a useful comparative indicator of development. Calculating according to Brown's rules (1973, p. 66) for the tapes of BRENDA I, (012) age 1;0.2 through (061) age 1;2.5, the MLU is 1.0. For BRENDA II the

TABLE 2. Facsimile Page of Transcription (from 141)

(B)	(Ch)	(Context)	(M)	(R)	(S)
121–123 t^h [hɛd] L (3x)			Ooh—Charlotte	Oop.	
124 [ɛ] CL	hehehe	Ch pushes B down—B bumps head.		Head? Let me see.	
		B continues to sit by wall bumping her head.		Oh—yeah. Didn't crack open. It didn't crack open. Poor Brenda—poor Brenda bumped her head. It hurt?	
260 125 [bəmp] L					
126 [hɛ] L			Charlotte, Mommy tired.	Yeah. What'd you bump? What'd you bump?	Mommy tired. Go to sleep.
127 [bəmp] Fx					
128 [bəmʔɛʔ] C			All right.		
129 [bəmʔːpʰːmi] L			Don't run away then.		
130 [bamp] Fx					
131 [bam] C				What'd you bump?	
270 132 [bam] L					
133 [bamʔ] Fx					
134 [tɛpʰ]F				Oh, don't. You're gonna hurt your head. (Laugh)	
135 [tɛpʰ]L				She threatens to step on my microphone.	
136 [tɛpʰ]L					

B. Brenda; Ch, Charlotte; M, Mother; R, Ron; S, Suzanne.

MLU does not yet rise above 1.0. In the last several sessions a few words have -*ing* which according to Brown's rules should be counted as a separate morpheme. However, in these cases, e.g. *hiding*, -*ing* does not appear to be productive since the form *hide* never appears without -*ing*. If -*ing* is counted the MLU for (141) would be 1.11. I feel 1.0 is more representative of the data.

For tape (161) age 1;10.17 several problems in counting arise. Again there is the problem of -*ing*. It still does not appear to be productive. A second problem is caused by words such as *tape corder*. Brown indicates that this should be counted as one morpheme. However, in this case both *tape* and *corder* appear independently. Of course, it is possible that there are three mono-morphemic words *tape*, *corder*, and *tapecorder*. For the sake of being complete the MLU's of (161) can be broken down as follows:

(1) MLU 1.28 if -*ing* counts ∅, *tape corder* counts 1.
(2) MLU 1.34 if -*ing* counts ∅, *tape corder* counts 2.
(3) MLU 1.46 if -*ing* counts 1, *tape corder* counts 1.
(4) MLU 1.52 if -*ing* counts 1, *tape corder* counts 2.

In future references to the MLU of (161), I will use (3) 1.46 as the MLU since this is the one derived from a literal reading of Brown's rules and is likely to compare best with other investigators. Finally, for (171) age 2;0.12 the MLU is 2.29.

II.2.2.8 Summary

Tape recordings were made of one thirty-minute period each week for a ten-week period (BRENDA I, age 1;0 to 1;2) and then later for an eight-week period (BRENDA II, age 1;7 to 1;8), and these two main periods of study were followed up at two-month intervals. The full thirty minutes of each tape were transcribed phonetically for Brenda and orthographically (with some modifications) for the others. The transcription was made within the same day or, at the latest, the following day. The data transcribed in this way were keypunched onto computer data cards for computer sorting. At this point my selection has included a phonetic transcription of Brenda's speech (both unintelligible and intelligible), an indication of intonation contour, notes on context, and all other speech in orthographic notation. This first-level selection has excluded any sounds that did not get recorded on the tapes and any information about context that was not written into notes or that is not recoverable from the sounds on tape. In the transcriptions, the exact pitch of utterances is not included nor is the phonetic shape of the adult utterances. These are recoverable, however, since they are recorded on the tapes. The original tapes, the handwritten transcriptions, and the computer print-outs are the three main types of data on which this study is based.

II.3   Second-Level Selection

It is common in the literature on child language to find the use of apparently unconscious techniques of filtering the data to be studied so that the data will ultimately be amenable to the investigator's own intuitions. These techniques form a kind of filter between the primary data and the data accepted for study, the effect of which is to severely restrict before study anything that is outside the investigator's competence—or, to be fair, I should say—extended competence.

II.3.1   Filtering of Data

Most of the now standard sources on child langauge have used some means of filtering the data of the study before analysis. In the earlier diary studies, this has been inevitable because of the limitations of handwritten notes. Anyone who has transcribed a tape recording of speech is aware of the many repetitions that are necessary before the transcription represents the full detail of the original. Leopold (1953, 1971, p. 135) complains that child language has only "engaged the marginal attention of linguists. Too often their references to it have been casual and, on closer inspection, erroneous. The obvious requirement that reliable data must be collected before conclusions are drawn has too often been neglected." Oscar Block is quoted in Jakobson (1968, p. 19) as saying he was able only to "slightly observe" and "record little." Block continues, "Not only is it difficult indeed to grasp and to record the sounds that are produced, but to interpret them also entails large demands." The most recent examples of this inevitable filtering in diary studies are the studies of Braine (1963), in which the parents' notes are taken as the primary data, and the somewhat shocking recent study of Olmsted (1971). The active use of a filtering technique has never been more explicitly stated than by Olmsted (p. 59):

> It had to be decided by the investigator whether the child's vocalizations were recognizable as attempts to say something in the language or not .... If the utterance was understandable to the investigator no interruption occurred, but if it was ambiguous, she would indicate by gesture (usually raised eyebrows) her state of indecision; then the mother would interpret the utterance if it was interpretable. If she did not find it interpretable, it was regarded as babbling, and plays no further part in this project.

In all of the cases mentioned here the selection of data took place at the time of recording. As a result, whatever was not selected is not recoverable. Sarles (1972, p. 67) has summarized this approach this way: "The decision concerning what to look at or consider, and what to throw out is usually made on a priori grounds which happen to fit into a given tradition."

In some studies, a second type of filtering took place after the tape recording of data. In Cazden's (Brown et al. 1968, 1971, p. 404) study of expansions, it is reported that "the tapes were transcribed by a secretary who was trained by a linguist on our staff and who was ignorant of the treatment assignment of the children." Another familiar example is Bloom's (1970, p. 17) explicit exclusion from analysis of "utterances that were wholly or partially unintelligible," "fragments of songs, rhymes or stories," as well as duplications and repetitions. Brown (1973, p. 56) reviews the process of selection of his group in which "713 consecutive complete utterances" were selected for analysis. In an earlier discussion (p. 42), Brown has made it clear that a complete utterance is, in fact, a sentence. In this case, then, everything that is not a sentence is being explicitly disregarded. It is important to note, however, that this type of filtering is not irrevocable. Brown points out that he was "continually discovering new kinds of information that could be mined from a transcription of conversation." (Brown, 1973, p. 53)

The attempt to determine the child's own system is perpetually frustrated by the fact that we have no access to intuitions about it. Of course, the method of study is to refer to adult intuitions as a means of breaking the closed circle of the child's system, and this amounts to the imposition of a kind of filter. This inevitable filtering is justifiable to the extent that the investigator is aware of it and does not allow it to operate any more than absolutely necessary. What I have found objectionable in many studies of child language is the imposition of filtering techniques at the stage of recording the data. In these cases, utterances of the child have been disregarded because they did not overlap in some immediately intelligible way with the linguist's system. In my work I have found that although at first I could not fully understand Brenda's utterances, my understanding could be "stretched" by reference to context or the developmental history of a word, and in these cases things that at the first look were unintelligible would become intelligible at a second look.

II.3.2   Intelligibility

In the data of BRENDA II, I found that for many utterances I could assign a "gloss." That is, I could recognize an adult English word that was very close to Brenda's word in both appropriateness of usage (as seen by its place in the context) and in phonetic shape. These utterances are commonly taken by adults as being attempts at adult words. Brown (1973, p. 106) has suggested that this amounts to taking "the parental rather than the behavioristic view of child speech." In making these glosses, I was using the technique that Bloom (1972, p. 28) has outlined as follows:

> What I did was to make the decision that I could have some idea of what the child meant by what he said, not that I could reach the *meaning* of a particular utterance. But I could make a *judgment* about the semantic intent that underlies particular utterances that children make, and that I could do this by relying on clues from the context and behavior in speech events. So that rather than simply looking at and recording only what the child said, I also took into consideration what it is he was talking about and made certain inferences about the semantic intent that underlies what he is talking about.

I did this assignment of glosses only after all the tapes of BRENDA II were collected and transcribed. I found that for the eight sessions the intelligibility of Brenda's utterances improved considerably with them. Table 3 gives the percentages and actual figures for each tape. In the first session of BRENDA II (071), 45

TABLE 3. Unintelligible Utterances

Tape	Unintelligible/ Total Utterances	Percent Unintelligible
071	213/387	59.0
081	122/318	38.4
091	92/356	25.8
101	81/430	18.8
111	107/551	19.4
121	58/276	20.8
131	78/332	23.5
141	50/325	15.4

percent were intelligible, whereas in the eighth session (141) 84.6 percent were intelligible. Even accepting a wide margin of error on my part and Brenda's, there is a clear difference between these sessions. This, of course, is what we would expect for a normally developing child.

I found out in this assignment of glosses, however, that some utterances that were unintelligible to me at first later became intelligible. There are two types of information that make this possible. The first is information about the context and the second is the developmental history of a word. These two types of information are not clearly separable, however, since the developmental history of a word becomes a part of its context. Several examples should make this clearer.

(091)44 dæʔkʰɔ̧
               (R)   Duck?
    45 dakʰ
    46 šɪm
    47 šɪm
    48 šɪm
    49 šɪm

In this first example, utterance 44 is marginally intelligible. Utterance 45 indicates that my guess was right—that is, 45 was said as confirmation. 46–49, by further expanding the context of *duck* to *swim*, added semantic confirmation to the phonetic confirmation. This kind of interaction was very frequent between Brenda and other speakers. It is, perhaps, the primary natural means of establishing glosses. (For further discussion, see V.6.2.)

In some cases, Brenda used a word which was either unknown to me, or I had no knowledge that Brenda knew the word. *Otemba* is the Japanese word for 'monkey'. At the time of (091) I did not know the word. As Brenda climbed up on a settee, she said (091)226 [tʰɛmbə] 227 [tʰɪmbə]. I transcribed these two utterances and, then, during the next visit I asked the mother if she knew the word. The mother said it was Japanese for 'monkey' and explained that Brenda always said *otemba* when she was climbing. In (131) a confirming example was recorded.

(131)	315	tʰɛmbəʔ	(B "climbs" tree while M holds her in position)
	316	tʸɛmba	
			(M) Otemba.
	317	məŋkʰi	
	318	məŋkʰi	
			(R) Who's the monkey?
	319	mi	
	320	mi	

In this example *otemba* was a word I did not know at first, and, for that reason, it was unintelligible to me without the additional context of the mother's explanation. In the next example *sick* was familiar enough but a combination of phonetic instability and a context in which the use of *sick* could not be established with certainty made utterances 128–130 quite unintelligible to me.

(071)	124	pitibebii	(B is holding a doll)
	125	bebi	
	126	pʰæk	
	127	pʰɪkụ	
	128	š	
	129	šɪkε̦	
	130	sɪk	
	131	bi	

The following sequence of utterances recorded a week later

(081) indicate that Brenda knew the word *sick* at that time. Further, the mother reported then that Brenda often pretended that she or her doll were sick or hurt and would go to the mother for medical attention. The acceptable remedy was usually a piece of Band-Aid tape over the spot indicated by Brenda.

(081)	166	tʰipʰ	'tape'	(B points to Band-Aid on her leg)
	167	tʰipʰ	'tape'	
	168	bwɪndah	'Brenda'	
	169	hɔto	'hurt'	
	170	maĩʔĩ	'Mommy' ('my'?)	
	171	maĩʔĩ	'Mommy'	
	172	bænĩʔĩ	'band-aid'	
	173	hɔʔtʰɪ̥	'hurt'	
	174	hɔʔ	'hurt'	
	175	x x x	?	
	176	hət	'hurt'	
	177	šɪkʰ	'sick'	
	178	šɪkʰ	'sick'	

On the basis of this use of *sick*, it becomes plausible to gloss (071) 128–130 as 'sick' as well. Both the phonetic shape and context are appropriate. That is, in the first use of *sick* (071) Brenda is saying that her doll (*pretty baby*) is sick. (126 and 127, however, remain unintelligible.)

The utterances (071) 128–130, [š.šɪ̥kᶒ.šɪk], give an example of a type of utterance sequence that is quite frequent. In these sequences, a target word is repeated until a reasonably acceptable form is achieved. This type of sequence is discussed in detail later (III.6.1). Here it is important to point out the similarity of this type of sequence, in which a word is repeated until the "best" form is pronounced, and the developmental history of a word. In some cases, the "best" form was not reached until a week or more later. In these cases, the early utterances could be established. One example (quoted in full in V.6.2) will illustrate this type of connection. On tape (111) [bəiš] is recorded nine times in sequence. I mistook this for *bicycle*, which Brenda told me was not correct. At the time of hearing the utterance, it was unintelligible. One week later Brenda said the following:

(121)49   brɛnda
    50   šipʰiʔ

           (M) Hm? Yeah, you thought lady
                 was wearing blanket, didn't you?

    51   baš
    52   baš

                 Yeah, on the bus, hm?
                 Yeah.

The story as reported by the mother is that she took Brenda to the doctor's office on the bus and that Brenda always sleeps on the bus. This accounts for Brenda's utterances. At the doctor's office, Brenda had seen a woman wearing a skirt of the same pattern as one of Charlotte's blankets. This accounts for the mother's reference to a blanket. In this case, the form [baš] can be quite clearly established as *bus*. Knowing this, it is not unreasonable to gloss [bəiš] as 'bus' on the tape (111) a week earlier, if the context would also support this gloss. Fortunately, these utterances were recorded on tape. When I listened again, I noticed that just before Brenda's nine repetitions of [bəiš], a motor vehicle of some kind can be heard passing in the street. It is probably this sound to which she is referring. At the time of recording and in making the initial transcription, I had missed the sound altogether.

The examples should be sufficient to demonstrate a number of ways in which the intelligibility of Brenda's utterances could be "stretched." Obviously, this intelligibility on the basis of phonological extrapolation and newly acquired contextual evidence can never be as secure as the immediate intelligibility of more mature forms well supported by immediate context. However, it becomes clear that at least some of the forms that might have been thrown out as nonlinguistic errors or "babbling" or noises are in fact systematic. And, of course, there is no telling how many more of the fifteen percent in the last tape (141) and the much larger percentage of the first tape (071) are in fact systematic but remain outside my ability to recover them by expansion of my own system, or how many would be understood if the boundaries of this study had been made slightly larger by increasing my knowledge of Brenda's development through such means as videotaping (to increase contextual references) or taping for longer sessions (thereby increasing the chances of finding a word in a variety of contexts).

Bowerman (1973) has also discussed this "stretching" of the investigator's understanding. She found that at first she had some difficulty understanding one child, Seppo. Bowerman says (p. 18) that "after some tutoring from her mother, however, I became familiar with her style of word alteration and was usually able to understand her."

Smith (1973), on the other hand, has effectively excluded all initially unintelligible utterances from his study by choosing not to tape record. He says (p. 10 FN2): "The use of a tape-recorder is not as helpful as might be expected. It is no use having a perfect recording of [ġʌk], if you do not know whether it corresponds to the adult *dog*, *duck*, *luck*, *truck*, or *stuck*." My point is just contrary to this—that it is important to have such utterances recorded because the investigator at the time of recording is simply not capable of understanding everything he is hearing, and some utterances of this type can be understood later.

II.3.3 The Utterance

A traditional bugaboo of linguistic studies has been the clear definition of an utterance. In the early stages of my study it was not a problem. Brenda's utterances were almost all one or two syllables bounded by considerable stretches of silence. There were a few in the data of BRENDA I that were long singing-like strings but even these were reasonably clearly defined.

In BRENDA II it was not always so clear. A number of times there was a close sequence of words that I classed as separate utterances. However, these were, in fact, said in one breath group (as far as I could tell from the tapes), and on either side there was silence. In contrast (141) 129 [bəm ʔ : pʰ·mi], *bump me*, included within one utterance a fairly long silence and possibly even a breath.

It became clear to me that my idea of an utterance was not that classically desired objective utterance of the speaker's competence but rather an extension of my adult English competence. I had classed successive instances of the word 'Brenda' as separate utterances no matter how closely they followed each other because in my speech 'Brenda Brenda Brenda' is not a sentence. On the other hand, I did take (141)129 as a single utterance because my extended competence can accept *bump me* as a child's paraphrase for my 'I bumped myself'.

I cannot say whether this has made any real difference in this study, although I can imagine some differences it might make. If only complex utterances were accepted for syntactic study, (141)129 would be accepted, whereas if separated into three separate utterances it would not. The domain often accepted by linguists for study is the sentence—which on the whole is taken as equivalent to the utterance. In this study, particularly in the section on constructions (Section III), this domain has been extended considerably.

To divide Brenda's speech into utterances, and study only separate utterances, imposes some restrictions on admissibility for study that may really be very natural. After all, if the child's langauge only becomes communicative to the extent that adults understand it, perhaps we should only want to study that part of it that is immediately communicative. This has been the almost unconscious approach of child language development studies up to now. On the other hand, if we want to get a fuller idea of what the child's competence is at any stage we need to severely restrict any prestudy systematicization. Fortunately for this study, Brenda's speech didn't reach the complexity that would have called for a whole scale investigation of this problem. I have grouped very few longer strings as single utterances. I have not made the utterance the criterion for admissibility to the study. I have tried to look at the larger speech event and place the whole set of utterances within this context for study.

II.4   The Uses of Context in this Study

Diesing (1971, p. 277) has said in his study of method in the social sciences,

> Scientists react to the weaknesses of a method (and all methods have weaknesses) in two different ways. If they are not using the method themselves, they cite its weaknesses as sufficient justification for ignoring the method and its results, for despising it as unscientific or inadequate, and for not allowing their students to learn it. If they are using the method, its weaknesses become problems, challenges that make work interesting and results an achievement.

In this study I have chosen to take the inevitable dependence on performance data as a challenge. I feel that the results of having used the method I have used are sufficiently interesting and important to justify having used it. As Diesing says somewhat later in the same work (p. 286), "One consideration that induces the holist to persevere in using his method despite its weaknesses and despite the slanders heaped on it is his feeling that it gets at something real that other methods miss." I feel that vertical construction is something real, and it is through the method of this study that it has come to light.

When I speak of "context," there are several things that might be understood. In this study I can isolate three more or less different types of context. Before treating them specifically, though, I want to point out that in referring to context one is also exercising his own intuitions of what constitutes context. That is, in this study for each type of context I used, there were some corresponding intuitions on my part about that context. I will try to make clear the intuitions of which I am aware after I describe the uses I have made of context.

I have said that there are three types of context for an utterance. They are (1) the surrounding utterances (linguistic context), (2) the nonlinguistic situation, and (3) the communicative overlap between the child and the investigator. I have made much of the first type in this study. Bloom (1970) introduced the full use of the second type, and virtually all studies have relied on the third type.

The first type of context amounts to the speech of the child or other speakers that immediately precedes or follows any single utterance of a child. My description of vertical constructions is entirely based on considering some of these sequences of utterances to be related. In addition to vertical construction, my discussion of repetitions as well as decisions about imitations and spontaneous utterances depends entirely on knowing what utterances have preceded. Finally, I have been able to decide about the intelligibility of some utterances on the basis of the utterances that precede or follow it. For instance, in the *mama . . . shoe* example, [šɪš] by itself might be wholly unintelligible, but, in the context of the string which leads up to the fairly intelligible [šuʔ], [šɪš] can be understood as *shoe*.

A second type of context is the nonlinguistic setting of an utterance. In the example just mentioned, the fact that Brenda is holding up her mother's shoe aids one's understanding of the utterances considerably. This might be called a referential use of context. The nonlinguistic setting is also important in determining the semantic relations of constructions. This, in particular, is the use to which Bloom (1970) has put knowledge of context.

The third type of context to which I have referred is the communication overlap between the child and the investigator—in this case Brenda and me. What I mean by this is that I have brought to the study a group of assumptions about the language and culture of the child I am studying. I assume, for instance, that whatever she says, it is reasonable for me to take it as Standard English, Hawaiian English, or perhaps, Japanese. Or again, I assume that Brenda's knowledge of the world will not range outside of Hawaiian-American culture. I think it is clear that assumptions of this sort do form a context within which the entire study is carried out and that they are the general background present in any particular speech situation.

I have made crucial use of at least six major intuitions in this study. To begin, I assumed that sounds that were bounded by silence represented whole utterances. It should be remembered that at the beginning of this study the silence boundaries were fairly long, but the intonation contour by which later utterances are marked had not developed. Later, the utterances were also marked by the adult intonational pattern. On the basis of that marking, then, the more complex utterances of the later period could be determined. At the first, however, I had to simply assume that silence represented word boundary.

A second kind of intuition was employed in making decisions about repetitions and different words. For example, in (051) [nene . nene . awau .] I took the first two utterances to be the same word but the third utterance to be a different word. I have no criterion for this decision other than my intuition about phonetic similarity of the first two and the difference from the third.

My decisions about imitation are related to the second intuition. Again, I have no objective criteria for telling how close a suspected imitation must be to the imitated form to be called a true imitation. I simply had to refer to intuitions about similarity.

The fourth and fifth intuitions are closely related. I have said that I could do such things as gloss Brenda's utterances on the basis of context. This assumes that my understanding of context is similar to hers. In this I feel dependence on intuitions that would be highly unreliable if we did not largely share our culture. The second problem in making glosses is that the context is not always very clear. In many cases, the assignment of a gloss was made on the basis of a high degree of phonetic similarity either to the adult form or to Brenda's form at some other point where the context was clear.

Finally, there is the use of intuitions in deriving word classes for grammatical analysis. The problems involved with this type of intuition will be discussed later in this study (VIII.1.1).

The reader may wonder what is the point of this confession. I am not the first investigator to use these intuitions, and I have not proposed any way of avoiding their use. The point I want to make is that the use of the investigator's intuitions makes a difference depending upon where in the study the intuition is applied. A widespread use of some of the intuitions I have mentioned at the time of recording the data would highly prejudice the study. I found, for instance, that my ability to understand utterances could be enhanced with the addition of certain kinds of knowledge. If I had set as my purpose to study only intelligible utterances and made the selection of them at the time of recording (as must inevitably happen in diary studies), the amount of data would be greatly limited and the type of data would be limited to only those utterances that are most immediately intelligible.

In general, my method was to restrict as much as possible the exercise of my intuitions while in the process of recording. I continued this restriction as much as possible in making the transcriptions. At the time of making the analysis, however, I found the use of intuitions to be fruitful in understanding the child's language. And since at this stage decisions are not irrevocable, I could entertain hypotheses without altering the data base upon which the conclusions ultimately rested.

II.4.1 Summary of Methodological Innovations

In this study I have used three types of data that have been excluded from other studies: One-word utterances, repetitions, and unintelligible utterances. These three types of data are crucial to my argument for the importance of vertical construction. In the first place, most of the data come from the "one-word" period—a period that has largely been ignored except by studies of phonology. In the second place, I have used repetitions as an important indicator of development as well as an indicator of complexity in production. In the third place, I have found that with experience of the child's world and developing phonological system I was able to "stretch" my understanding so that utterances which were at first hearing unintelligible became quite defensibly intelligible. It was on the basis of a number of these utterances that I first noticed vertical constructions. It is also true that because of the complexity introduced by vertical construction the phonetic shape of some of the words was affected. This had considerable importance in pointing up the constructional nature of the whole.

SECTION II

Background for Vertical Construction

CHAPTER III

Phonology

III.1 BRENDA I, First Session (012), Age 1;0.2

As an approach to the phonology of BRENDA I, two sessions, the first (012) [session (011) was recorded without Brenda as a participant for comparison to later sessions in which she was a participant: see II.2.1] and the eighth (051), have been selected for detailed study. Although this neglects mention of the intervening sessions, it will demonstrate both the method I have used for all of the tapes and some general developments.

At the first session (012), Brenda's mother reported that she knew only a few words. They were "dada," "maman," "doll," "flower," and "nene." The mother then tried to prompt Brenda to say some of them by pointing to things and saying "What's that?" On the whole, Brenda did not respond much to this prompting.

III.1.1 Utterance Types

Brenda made 66 utterances on tape (012). In addition to these 66, there was a stretch of about thirty seconds during which she cried. No attempt was made to transcribe her crying. The 66 utterances can be broken into six groups or types as follows:

(1) Baby talk. There was a group of 22 utterances that varied from [ne:ne:] (the most frequent phonetic shape) to [nə] and [e:nen]. The mother reported these to be Brenda's approximations for

nennen, a Japanese baby talk form for "sleep" and, in Brenda's speech, 'milk', 'juice', 'baby bottle', and maybe 'mother'. This was the most common form used (one-third of the total), and Brenda was able to use it in two ways. She used it in the presence of the bottle, apparently to refer to it. She also used it when there was no bottle with the result of getting the mother to give her some more milk. In Chapter 9, I have considered the first use to be the speech act of reference. The second I considered to be a directive.

(2) Brenda originals. Utterances 53 through 58 demonstrate this type.

(012) 53   awawawa
      54   a:ba
      55   awa
      56   a:
      57   æl^n
      58   æ:

These utterances were accompanied by crawling toward the microphone on the floor and finally pushing it away. Brenda then went to the mother and raised her arms to indicate she wanted to be carried. When the mother picked her up she waved goodbye to me. It would be highly speculative to try to assign any adult gloss to this group of utterances. 'Away' might be suggested. The development of the form ⟨awəu⟩ later in BRENDA I largely with the meaning of 'I want' or 'again' might indicate a meaning of this sort here, even though the semantics of this situation is more the negative 'I don't want'. The point to be made is that there is probably no adult word or sentence to which this form of Brenda's corresponds. Or if there is, there is no way of knowing what it might be. It seems more plausible to say that it is original with her, that she has invented an utterance to accompany actions of desiring or rejection, i.e., a type of directive. This type occurred 9 times in (012).

(3) Approximation of adult word. Utterances 21 and 22 demonstrate this type. The mother is holding Brenda. Brenda looks at a small doll on top of the television and says,

(012) 21   da: (whispered)
      22   da: (loud)

Since there was no *immediately* preceding attempt to prompt Brenda to say *doll*, it may be a spontaneous naming of the object. (But see V.2.) The phonetic form is both stable for the two utterances and recognizable to adults as corresponding to the adult word. This is probably a reference.

(4) Imitations. An example of this type occurred when the mother said, "That's a Hakata doll," and Brenda said,

(012) 10   ka:

It should be pointed out that the mother's "Hakata" carried heavy stress on the second syllable, which seems to be what Brenda was imitating.

(5) Long singing utterances. There were two of these, 28 and 49. Utterance 28 was the longest with 15 syllables. (On the basis of the absence of final consonants in the predominant short utterances, I have used a CV structure as my working definition of a syllable.)

(012) 28   pa:lælænəbætænætagabatwagzæzæzæ

This was in marked contrast to all of the other types. Of the total of 66 utterances only ten were longer than two syllables: Five of those were three syllables, three were four syllables. The justification for calling these two long utterances "singing" was the intonation patterns and the context. The mother had told us a story about how Charlotte had seen a man on television singing into a microphone and said that he was singing into an egg. The context of 28 was my saying, "Do you know what this is? It's not an egg." I held out the microphone toward Brenda, and it seems as if she then tried to sing. She then looked first at the television and then at the piano.

(6) The others. It is not surprising that the miscellany should include 30 utterances—almost half of what Brenda said. It is simply impossible to be assertive about these since there is little contextual evidence to place them in any of the groups above. They can be described though as being less regular—that is, both in the sense that they occur mostly as isolated utterances with no repetitions and in the sense that the phonetic variation is wider than for the first three groups noted above. The phonetic variation does not,

however, go outside a fairly delimitable area. In the discussion to follow, what is said about Brenda's system is to be understood as including this unintelligible miscellany as well. The speech act functioning will be discussed in more detail in Chapter 9.

III.1.2   Words

Up to now I have avoided calling any of Brenda's utterances words. Before doing that we need some definition of "word." For the purposes of this study, I take "word" to mean a systematic matching of meaning and form. Later, when the forms become more complex, it becomes a problem to make a distinction between utterances that are words and utterances that at some higher level are constructions made up of words. About the same time, the problem of the discrimination of the elements of which words are made up emerges. For this early stage, however, there seems little need to try to distinguish different levels of form and different levels of meaning. For Brenda's system it seems that some of her "words" correspond to adult sentences, some of them to adult words. It is this apparent lack of distinction that has led me to the very general definition above of Brenda's "word" being any systematic matching of meaning and form. This definition of word corresponds well with Halliday's (1973b) "posture."

III.1.3   Determination of Form — Phonetic Variability

The traditional means of determining to what extent phonetic variation is allophonic variation is to ask for a "same or different" judgment from the informant: That is, to vary the form and ask if the meaning remains the same. This seems to be out of reach for an investigator working with very young children. Meaning is not reported but only inferred by the investigator from the context. Utterances like (012) 53–58 become very important in determination of form.

(012) 53   awawawa
    54   a:ba
    55   awa
    56   a:
    57   æl^n
    58   æ:

We have to assume that the child in the succession of utteránces is repeating herself. This does not appear to be an important assumption, perhaps, until this same context is later invoked as being evidence for construction. If we accept that assumption, then we can say that the variation between [w] and [b] in 53 and 54 is not significant. We are further accepting that the reduplication is also not significant. We can see that the variation between [a] and [æ] and finally between [w], [b], and [lⁿ] is not significant. This gives us our first step toward understanding Brenda's system.

Carrying out the same procedure for another form, ⟨nene⟩ we find that [e] varies with [ɛ] and [æ], but that [n] varies only in length, and that this word with two exceptions is always in the reduplicated form.

Finally, for Brenda's third word "doll" we find no variation. It appears twice as [da:].

III.1.4   Homophony or Semantic Variation

On the other side of the definition, once we have found the limits of phonetic variation for a particular word in a more or less definite context, how do we consider phonetically similar utterances in which the context is unclear or actually different? Brenda's most common word in this session was ⟨nene⟩. It occurred with considerable regularity in places where it could mean 'milk', 'juice', 'sleep', 'mother', or maybe other things, since it also occurred where no specific content could be determined. In this case it seems reasonable to think that this is one word with a wide range of meanings—all of them certainly related and of central importance to an infant's world. 'Nurture' would, perhaps, be a reasonable gloss of the semantic space of this word. We would expect then to see the process of development as a process of the successive differentiation of both forms and meanings.

III.1.5   Brenda's Words

The surest way to determine meaning is by reference to a clear context. This has pointed to the use of forms that are repeated in a constant context as the best way to look at phonetic variability. Further, the spontaneity of an utterance is useful in separating Brenda's productive system from her ability to imitate. These two factors limit the study of Brenda's phonology to the study of her

most frequent words. These words can be checked against other
forms but it is difficult to say anything about the systematicity of
isolated forms—especially when the context cannot be well
established.

For these reasons, we can then refer to Brenda's words at
BRENDA I as being those forms that occur at least frequently
enough to be checked against each other for variability of phonetic
shape and in varying contexts for range of meaning. We can see,
then, that of the six types of utterances given above (1), (2), and
(3) can reasonably be considered to be words. The others are either
not words or can only be tentatively considered as such. In the
first session (012) Brenda has three words that make up slightly
more half the total. These words are ⟨nene⟩ ('milk', 'juice', 'bottle',
'mother', 'sleep'—i.e., 'nurture'). ⟨awa⟩ ('I don't want', 'I reject'),
and ⟨da⟩ ('doll'). These spellings are not to be taken as phonemi-
cizations but rather approximations of the most common form.
This type of spelling is indicated by angle brackets (⟨ ⟩).

III.2   BRENDA I, Eighth Session (051), Age 1;1.22

By the eighth session, Brenda's system has begun to expand.
There are a total of 183 utterances. Out of this total of 183, we can
distinguish eight words that account for 153 utterances. The
remaining 30 utterances are in the categories of imitated words
and unintelligible utterances that may or may not be words.

III.2.1   Methodology

Several of these words deserve detailed study since they point
up some methodological considerations. The most common word
again is ⟨awəu⟩. It occurs 49 times—that is, more than one-fourth
of the total. What follows is a selection of instances of this word
and the context in which it occurred. In several cases the mother's
response is included. Those utterances blocked together shared the
same context.

(051)2	awʌ	(Playing with ice cubes)
8	avau	(Reaching out to grasp Suzanne's necklace)
11	awa	(Reaching for necklace again)

27	awə	(Trying to pick up ice cube)
28	æwəu	
29	awəu	
33	avə	(Reaching for Suzanne's necklace)
34	awa	
35	dævəu	
36	æwəu	
37	æwə	
38	ævə	(No specific context can be determined)
39	avə	
40	æla	
53	ala	(Looking at pictures of food in book—
54	ælə	sausage, etc.)
55	æyɨ	
		(M) You want?
134	avu	(Reaches out and grasps necklace)
135	avə	
136	avə	
137	ævəu	
138	aw	
139	æləu	
140	æwəu	
141	awə	
171	nʔ	(Tries to take off shoe)
172	awə	(M) You want it off?
		O. K.
173	nʔ	
174	awə	(Gets shoe off and throws it away from her)
		(M) You don't like it.

The meaning that was suggested for ⟨awa⟩ in the first session can be seen more clearly now by the context in which this word occurs. On two different occasions it accompanies Brenda's attempts to pick up ice cubes. On three different occasions Brenda says this word as she reaches to grasp Suzanne's necklace. On the other two occasions the mother responds to this as if Brenda has said she wants something. In the last two instances it appears to be an action Brenda wants—that the shoe be taken off. It seems reasonable to consider the meaning of this word to be quite close to that expressed by the adult form ":I want." The phonetic similarity, of course, is striking.

The following frequent words pose some problems. First a group of examples will be given and the discussion will follow.

		(R) What's this?
(051)26	dæyi	(R hands B the Hakata doll)
30	devəu	(B holds doll in hands)
31	dævlə	
32	dæwə	
46	edi	(Looking at magazine picture of woman's face)
47	dedi	
48	dædi	
49	dædi	
50	dædi	
51	dedi	
52	dædi	
61	dædi	(Picks up magazine—it is Daddy's magazine)
111	dau	(Spills juice while drinking and
112	dawu	looks down on floor)
169	dæyu	(S gives B doll)
178	dædi	(M) Daddy? Daddy not here.
179	dedi	Where's Daddy?
		Uh? huh? Where?
180	edi?	
		Daddy at work.
181	dæyi	
		Uh huh.
182	dæd	
		Hai. Hai. (Japanese *yes*)

183   ædiˀi

Uh huh. Every morning she
wants to go out with Daddy.

What is being questioned here is whether there is one word
or more than one word in the examples above. One would like to
think that Brenda has two words, ⟨dædi⟩ ('daddy', 'picture in a
magazine', 'baby'—on the basis of the previous session) and ⟨dæyu⟩
('down', 'doll'). In the case of the first word there would be the
problem of homophony since it is hard to imagine grouping *daddy*
and *baby* and pictures in a magazine semantically. However, on
the basis of the dialogue between Brenda and the mother we see
that for the mother, at least, [dædi], [dedi], and [dæyi] are all taken
to be the same word with varying form. If this represents successive
instances of the same word, then the two groups have to be classed
together. It is plausible that 181 is either an error of some kind or
that the mother takes it wrong. Since it is the only instance of the
[y] occurring where we would expect [d] an error is not unlikely.
Also the fact that the dialogue goes on and on without any evidence
that Brenda feels she is being understood may indicate that she
was either saying something other than *daddy* or that she was making
an attempt to get these words clarified by intentionally violating
her phonemicization to see what would happen. Whatever the
reason, it seems that the most plausible solution is to consider
these utterances as two separate words.

III.2.2   Brenda's Words

In session eight (051) Brenda has the following eight words.
The spellings, again, are not to be taken as phonemic or phonetic
but rather as the most frequent phonetic shape.

Word	Frequency	Meaning
awəu	49	I want, don't want
nau	29	no
dædi	22	daddy, baby, picture in magazine
dæyu	16	down, doll
nene	14	liquid food
e	10	yes
mæmə	7	solid food
ada	6	other, another

III.3   Jakobson's Stages

Since Jakobson's (1968) introduction of the concept of distinctive contrast to studies of child phonology, a number of investigators have voiced general support for his claims. (For example, Velten, 1943, 1971; Leopold, 1953, 1971). In general they have agreed that the development of phonology proceeds in a series of stages marked by successively finer contrasts. It is important now to discuss the system of BRENDA I in light of these stages.

To begin it is clear that Brenda at tape (012) age 1;0.2 is within the stage of "the first acquisition of words" (Jakobson 1968, p. 21). This is the starting point of Jakobson's stages. The first stage for Jakobson is that in which the maximum distinction between consonant and vowel is the only distinction. The second stage consists of a differentiation between two consonants, a nasal consonant and an oral consonant. The third stage brings a distinction in the consonants between a labial and a dental consonant. The following diagram illustrates these three stages using Brenda's most frequent phonetic segment as the representative. (It should be noted that the only formal meaning of *d* above in stage 1 is "consonant" and "forward." That Jakobson uses *p* to represent this is not in contrast with this use of *d*.)

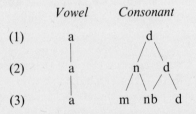

From Brenda's three words, we can determine that she is in the second stage for the first session (012). In these three words we have clear evidence of a nasal/oral split in the consonants. Brenda has ⟨nene⟩ (sometime [ne]) and ⟨da⟩. There is no evidence for the further split of stage 3, i.e., there is no word *⟨meme⟩ nor *⟨ba⟩. A strict phonemicization, then, in Jakobsonian terms would give /nana/, ada/, and /da/ for Brenda's three words, where *n–d* represents only a contrast of nasality and *a*, any vowel that is not forward.

Jakobson's stage 2 allows two contrasts, nasal/oral (for consonants) and consonant/vowel (for segments). At this stage, the forward/back contrast parallels the consonant/vowel contrast so that all consonants are forward and all vowels are back. Jakobson also assumes a word structure of CV or (in reduplication) CVCV. These restrictions would allow only the four words /da/, /na/, /dada/, and /nana/. We can assume Brenda's ⟨nene⟩ and ⟨da⟩ match Jakobson's /nana/ and /da/, respectively. ⟨dada⟩, which was reported by the mother (but did not appear on tape), matches /dada/. This leaves Jakobson's /na/ unaccounted for. This matching also does not account for Brenda's ⟨awa⟩.

Of course, because a structure such as /na/ is possible does not mean the child has to have a word that makes use of it. It is even possible that such a word did exist but simply did not occur in my data. The other form, ⟨awa⟩, is somewhat more problematic since it is of a VCV structure. This implies a CVCV/VCV contrast, that is, a contrast between /dada/ and /ada/, and /nana/ and /ana/. This latter form, /ana/, does not occur.

The only conclusion is that Jakobson's stage 2 indicates the general nature of Brenda's system, but that if his claims are taken literally they are not substantiated in this analysis of Brenda's words.

III.3.1   Phonetic Conditioning

In discussing the variablility of the vowels, it was noted that in ⟨nene⟩ [e] varied with [ɛ] and [æ]. In ⟨awa⟩, however, [a] varied with [æ]. Jakobson's solution to this type of problem is to claim that there is no significant contrast among vowels at this stage. If this is the case, then the question of the phonetic conditioning is raised. It can be seen that [e] and [ɛ] only occur after the nasal. [æ] occurs in that position as well as before (l^n). [a] occurs after [d] and before [w]. This, then, points to the nasal being the condition for the raising and fronting of the vowel [a], which in my transcription is a low central vowel.

III.3.2   Jakobson's Stages in (051)

In looking at the eight words of tape (051), age 1;1.22, we can see that Brenda is now in the third stage but has not yet reached the fourth. It may be useful to recall the stages. The following diagram shows these stages through the fourth in which the wide vowel splits into a wide/narrow contrast.

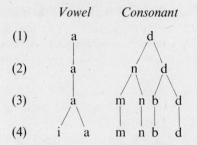

Evidence for the third stage can be seen in the contrast between 56 through 59 and 165 through 168 below.

(051) 56   m   (Looking at pictures of solid food
      57   mæ   in book, e.g., fish and French fries)
      58   məmæ
      59   mɛmæ

      165 nænæ   (Drinking juice from cup)
      166 nene
      167 nene
      168 n

These examples show a definite contrast between the labial and dental nasals accompanied by a semantic difference. The same split can be seen to have developed, although somewhat differently, for the nonnasal consonant. Many examples of ⟨awa⟩ have been given above. Below are some examples of the dental consonant.

(051)121   ab   (Brenda's cup leaked, and she held
      122   ada   it up asking for another)
      123   ada
      124   adða?

The first instance, 121, may or may not be a [b]. It is somewhat unclear on the tape. The following [d]'s, however, are clearer. It looks as if the stage 3, labial-dental split, seems to be not a contrast in position so much as a split between [+continuant] and [−continuant]. That is, where we would have the underlying labial, /b/, we see on the surface [w], [v], [y], and [l] (as in III.2.1 above). For /d/ we have [b], [d], [dð], and [ð] in one instance. As can be seen in the case of the nonnasal distinction, it is not as clear and definite as the nasal distinction nor as clear as Jakobson has claimed. Furthermore, what are we to make of the apparently real distinction between ⟨dædi⟩ and ⟨dæyu⟩? Jakobson makes no mention of glides at this stage. Perhaps on the basis of what we have seen for ⟨awa⟩, that is, that [w] and [y] are invariation, we may say that ⟨dæyu⟩ could be represented as /daba/. This would not cause any formal difficulties but would require us to believe that /daba/ could be the child's deep representation for the adult *down* or *doll*.

It could be argued that the third stage has not yet been reached. It could be said that the [b] in 121 is evidence that the split has not taken place. If the third stage has not been reached yet, then ⟨dædi⟩ and ⟨dæyu⟩ are in fact the same word. But so are ⟨mæmə⟩ and ⟨nene⟩. Jakobson's system of contrasts does not admit of successive approximation, and yet that looks like what is happening with Brenda's system. It appears that for nasal consonants she has reached the third stage in which there is a labial/dental contrast, but for nonnasals the contrast is in the process of being established. For the words ⟨awəu⟩ and ⟨ada⟩ there is a contrast of sorts. One of the meanings of ⟨dædi⟩ is 'baby', and, if the contrast were fully established, we would expect Brenda to begin saying something like [bebi]. However, if we look at the next week (052), Brenda has several words with a [b], for example, [ba] (looking at a balloon). As much as four weeks later (Sll), she is still insistently saying ⟨dedi⟩ for *baby*. By then, the third stage is definitely established, and the only explanation that can be put forward is that this particular world has remained as an idiomatic anachronism in Brenda's otherwise developing system.

III.4 Apparently Nonsystematic Words

It might be argued that Brenda's system is developed much beyond stage 3 and that examples that would be needed to establish Jakobson's stages simply did not occur in this half hour. If that is true, then any final analysis of any child's system will always be out of reach since there is no way to assure that one has been fortunate enough to uncover all the relevant examples. Jakobson's claims, however, are based on general principles that should be evident in any of the utterances available. For this reason, the analysis to this point has been of the few frequently repeated words.

A serious problem arises, however, in looking at a number of words that occur that neither fit the supposed phonemic system nor can be demonstrated to be imitation. The details of imitation will be discussed below (V.1). For now a small sample will illustrate the problem. In tape (021), Brenda says [čoda] (utterance 21). This corresponds well to the mother's Japanese *chodai* 'please give it to me'. There is no instance of this word anywhere on the tape before this. The phonetic clarity of the word as well as the appropriate usage (she was handing something to her mother) qualify it as a real word. Yet it seems to be well outside the ⟨awa⟩, ⟨da⟩, ⟨nene⟩ system of that period.

A second example is on tape (042)—23 [laulau]. The context for this is the presentation of a picture of flowers. No one in the preceding recorded context has said *flowers* so this can reasonably be thought to be Brenda's own word for flower. However, the supposed phonemic system would have no means of differentiating this surface form from ⟨dedi⟩ since at that time only a nasal/oral contrast of stage 2 and the labial/dental contrast of stage 3 can be assumed.

These are only a few selected from a larger group of words that seem to violate Jakobson's claims in two ways. In the first type, there is use of a word quite outside the phonological system that can be supposed for that period on the basis of the large group of more or less systematic words. In the second type, there are utterances within the phonological system but in which a distinction apparently quite advanced (e.g., the dental/liquid contrast) is used appropriately. These data present a dilemma. The system may be developed well beyond that supposed on the basis of the large group of frequent words. But it remains impossible to determine that system because of the impossibility of knowing if all the relevant items have been found. On the other hand, there may be a system such as Jakobson has claimed but within that system there is room for both non-systematic utterances (perhaps idioms) and successive approximation of later distinctions.

III.5   Conclusion to BRENDA I Phonology

To conclude this discussion of the phonology of BRENDA I we can definitely show that Jakobson's fourth stage has not been reached. In no case can we demonstrate a wide vowel/narrow vowel contrast. It does remain to be explained, however, how the [i] in

⟨dædi⟩ is consistently that vowel and no other. Also ⟨e⟩ 'yes' is always [e] and never [a] nor [æ]. In these cases phonetic conditioning is not a plausible explanation. This appears to be further evidence that, although there is no formal means of recognizing these consistencies in Jakobson's framework, there is nonetheless a preference for one noncontrastive segment over another in the child's system. It suggests that a conceptual framework that eliminates the concept of noncontrastive variation and successive approximation in fact is not representative of the developing system of a child in the process of learning a language.

Leopold (1953, 1971) has referred to this phenomenon as "pre-patterning." I have discussed it in some detail because I plan to show in the discussion of construction (VII.3.5) that this same type of successive approximation that is operating in phonology is paralleled in developments in construction. This parallelism of development indicates that "pre-patterning" or successive approximation is an active process throughout the language acquisition process rather than specific to any particular aspect.

III.6   Problems of Data in BRENDA II, Ages 1;7.2 to 1;8.21

In the discussion of data filtering (II.3.1), I raised several questions about how decisions are made in the selection of data for study. Here again, the same questions come up but in somewhat more interesting detail. They are basically two questions: (1) What is a word? and (2) what is the system under analysis?

III.6.1   What Is a Word ?

The idea of phonology is to reduce phonetic variation to some more basic set of elements and a set of rules relating them. To do this, some decision has to be made about the significance of surface variation; it is the "same or different" judgment. With a child as young as Brenda, one must be content with recurrences of the word in the same or similar contexts to decide if it is the same word. This does not solve all the problems, however, since sometimes a second decision has to be made about production variation which may not be the same as allophonic variation. Two examples from (071) will clarify the problem.

The first example is of the word *bear* that Brenda said while sitting on a toy bear.

(071)84 bæu
    85 biæu
    86 bʸæ

In this case, it is not difficult to consider these all the same word and that [b], [bi], and [bʸ] are in free variation, as well as [æ] and [æu]. The solution is as clear as one could hope for.

In the second example, the problem of production is added. Brenda picks up her mother's shoe and says:

(071)263 š
    264 šɪ
    265 š
    266 šɪš
    267 šu
    268 šuʔ
    269 šuš

            (S) Shoes!

    270 šɪ̥
    271 šɪ̥
    272 šuʔ

Once 268 is reached it is clear that Brenda is saying *shoe*. How far back in the string can one go saying that it is phonetic variation, and what is the difference between that and the earlier production difficulties? It seems clear that Brenda is trying to say *shoe* and finally succeeds. Of these ten utterances how many are words? Are there two strings of repetitions, 263 through 269 and 270 through 272, culminating in the "word" or is this a unified set of repetitions? Decisions of this sort are always tentative. On the basis of pauses (see V.6.1. for a fuller description of this type of sequence in the discussion of repetitions), it appears that 263 through 269 form a set and 270 through 272 form a second set. This seems to be true since in the first set Brenda needs seven repetitions to get the form pronounced well enough for Suzanne to understand. After Suzanne's "shoes," however, only three repetitions are needed to produce the "best" form. Furthermore, the whispered vowels of 270 and 271 indicate that Brenda may have been practicing the form softly before risking a full-voice pronunciation. This would suggest that even Brenda was aware of a difference between production variation and allophonic variation.

In a strict study of the phonology of a child's speech, then, we can only study forms that are intelligible in the first place, or which can be made intelligible by reference to context, and forms that we somehow judge to be free of production errors of the grossest type. What is left as the basic form of a word is what occurs most frequently, since that is our only basis for deciding. The words in this study of BRENDA II phonology are of this type in most cases. In Tables 5 and 6, the phonetic shape given is the best form that can be sifted out through this process. These forms correspond to the form given in angle brackets ($\langle \rangle$) for BRENDA I. It should be understood that the phonetic shape given may not be the only one that may have occurred for a word given. Important differences have been given in parentheses.

III.6.2   What Is the System under Analysis?

In a system as varying and as quickly changing as that of a one-year-old child, some important decisions are made at the point of selection of the system for study. A study of the data from the full eight weeks would show developmental changes of considerable magnitude, but since many of these changes are irreversible, one would not want to consider all of the data to constitute a stable system, that is, a synchronic system. On the other hand, there is no lower limit one can place on the length of time covered to guarantee that no developmental change will take place. This study has taken each half-hour session as an arbitrary synchronic whole and then looked at the development from week to week, particularly comparing the first session of BRENDA II (071) with the last session (141). This is the same technique that was used for BRENDA I.

In the course of eight half-hour tapes, Brenda made 2,940 utterances from which 319 words (types) can be identified. All of those words are not of equal value in a study of her phonology. Some of them are clearly more indicative of Brenda's own system than others. One means of deciding about Brenda's system is to look only at words that have occurred spontaneously. By separating these words from those that have followed another speaker's model, we can safely eliminate imitation as an immediate source of Brenda's words. A second means of establishing stability in the corpus studied is to look only at words that occur more frequently than in just one session. This would have the effect of eliminating any words that might be remembered from just before the taping session and were in fact not really a part of Brenda's system.

The two categories of spontaneity and occurrence in more than one session will cross classify four groups of data. They are given in order of importance. This is also the order of frequency.

(1) Spontaneous words that occur in more than one session.

(2) Spontaneous words that do not occur on any other tape.

(3) Modeled words that are repeated in later sessions as spontaneous words.

(4) Modeled words that do not recur.

The term "modeled" requires clarification. When I refer to one of Brenda's utterances as "modeled," I mean that it may have been imitated but that I am not willing to assert that it was. The difficulty of deciding whether an utterance is, in fact, an imitation is discussed in detail in V.2.1. "Modeled" means that a model for Brenda's utterance was present in the speech environment during the preceding five minutes. Obviously, Brenda may or may not have heard the model. If I call her utterance an "imitation," I have reason to believe that she did hear the model. I have used "modeled" to remain uncommitted. "Spontaneous" utterances are all those that are not "modeled."

The discussion that follows is a relatively context-free study of phonology. The very important questions of imitation and repetition that have been raised by the use of such terms as "spontaneity" and "modeled" have been deferred for fuller discussion in V.2.1 on discourse redundancies.

Appendix B gives data about this corpus. First, there is a list of the 118 words that were used in more than one session. With each word is listed the sessions in which it occurred. Then there is a list of the 201 words that occur in just one session along with the session number. Finally, there is a list of the most frequent words and the number of sessions in which each occurs.

III.7   BRENDA II, First Session (071), Age 1;7.2

At this first session, Brenda had changed considerably from the end of BRENDA I, age 1;1.22. About five months had passed since the last sessions of BRENDA I. The total number of utterances had doubled. There were five times as many different words. In (071) Brenda used 44 words (types). They can be broken down as above into four groups as follows:

(1) 23 spontaneous words that are later found in at least one other session.

(2) 12 spontaneous words that do not appear later.

(3)   5 modeled words that later appear as spontaneous words.

(4)   4 modeled words that do not reappear.

Table 4 is a list of these words by the four categories. The table gives the adult equivalent and the best phonetic shape for both spontaneous and modeled forms. Eleven of the thirty-five spontaneous words were said by an adult after Brenda's first use and then repeated again by Brenda. This is the reason these two forms are given.

TABLE 4. The Words of (071) Grouped by Category of Spontaneity

Gloss	Spontaneous Form	Modeled Form
I. Spontaneous Words that are repeated in later tapes		
1. baby (3)ᵃ	bebi (pẽ)	bebi
2. bear (5)	bʸæu (bæu, biæu, bʸæ)	—
3. bed (2)	bɛtʰ	—
4. big (2)	bek	bik
5. blue (2)	pu	bu
6. Brenda (8)	pʰɛntʰə	—
7. cookie (3)	kukʰi	—
8. daddy (6)	dædi (æ ~ e)	—
9. eat (5)	it	—
10. hat (4)	hæˀ	—
11. (hor)sie (6)	šiˀ	—
12. mama (6)	mama	—
13. mommy (8)	mami (ˀ)	—
14. nice	nəis	nəis
15. paper (5)	pʰeipʰ	—
16. pen (4)	p⁽ʰ⁾eyɛn	pʰæ̃ (æ ~ ai ~ ɛ) (æ̃n ~ æ̃ˀ)
17. see (3)	ušiˀ	ušiˀ
18. shoe (2)	šu	šuˀ
19. sick (2)	šɪk	—
20. swim (4)	šɛm(ˀ)	—
21. tape (6)	tʰeipči	tʰəiš, tʰeitʰ
22. walk (5)	wakʰ	—
23. wowow	wəwəu	—

TABLE 4—*Continued*

Gloss	Spontaneous Form	Modeled Form
II. Spontaneous Words that are not repeated in later tapes		
1. boat	bout^(h) (tʰ ~ ʔ)	—
2. bone	boni	—
3. Checkers	tʰe̥kʰo̥ ~ kʰe̥kʰo̥	—
4. corder	gɔdə̧ʔ	—
5. cut	kʰə̧ʔ	—
6. hankie	heŋgiʔ	—
7. I do	aidu	—
8. mother	maðə	—
9. net	nɛ	nɛ (ʔ) ~ næ
10. Pogo	pʰɔkʰɔ(ʔₕ)	pʰɔkʰɔʔo
11. Ralph	rəuš	—
12. you too	yutʰu	—
III. Modeled Words that are repeated in later sessions as Spontaneous		
1. climb (2)		kʰæmɔ̃
2. jump (3)		dəmə
3. orange (4)		awə
4. pencil (2)		pʰeh ʔšɪʔ
5. write (6)		rait
IV. Modeled Words that are not repeated in later sessions		
1. chameleon		liʔi
2. come		kʰəm
3. hand		hæ̃n
4. pussy		pʰuʔsiʔ

ᵃ The number in parentheses indicates the number of repetitions.

III.7.1   Stops in BRENDA II, Tape (071)

There is a three-way contrast in stops for place of articulation: labial, alveolar, and velar. There also appears to be a contrast either in voicing or aspiration but this distinction is not always clear. Looking first at the labials, we could assume underlying /b/ and /p/. On the surface, [b] is in free variation with [bʸ]. [p] is found in [pu], *blue*. It is also found in the position before consonants [č] or [tʰ]. [pʰ] is found in all the places one would expect it from adult phonology, except it also appears in the word *Brenda*. There are no [b]'s in final position. From this, we can see that although there is basically a distinction between /b/ and /p/ it is not maintained everywhere.

For alveolar stops, the situation is somewhat clearer. We could posit /d/ and /t/. There are no [d]'s in final position. Since there were also no [b]'s in this position, the question of word-final devoicing is raised. This will be taken up after the discussion of velars below. In other positions /d/ is always [d]. /t/ is found as [t] in variation with [tʰ] in final position. It is [tʰ] elsewhere except in one word, *Checkers*, where [tʰ] varies with [kʰ] in initial position. Notice that this variation is in the position where the adult system has [č].

It seems fairly clear from the fact that there is a contrast in voicing for all three points of articulation in all positions in the word except the final position that what is taking place is neutralization of voicing in final position. Since there is no morphological evidence at this early stage to give further evidence of neutralization, my final decision was based on a combination of the regularity of the contrast in other positions and by comparison with what is expected from the adult system.

III.7.2 Nasals in BRENDA II, Tape (071)

The nasals present the simplest and clearest segments in Brenda's system. We can assume /m/ and /n/ with one rule: that /n/ becomes [ŋ] before [g]. This is very much like the adult system. The modeled word, *pen*, is interesting. We see that there are two forms—[pʰæˀ] and [pʰæn]. In this case, a nasalized vowel/nasal sequence is in variation with a nasalized vowel plus [ˀ]. If this form is compared with the spontaneous form of the same word *pen* [pʰeyɛn], it can be seen that what has been changed is length. This is, perhaps, evidence for the status of [ˀ] as the least marked consonant, at least in final position. Under conditions of rapid speech or, in this case, an attempt to produce a single syllable in the place of two syllables, other consonants are reduced to [ˀ].

III.7.3 Fricatives in BRENDA II, Tape (071)

The only regular fricatives in Brenda's use are [š] and [s]. These could be assumed to be underlying /š/ with [s] occurring word final. There is one exception—which occurs in the word *Ralph*. The final consonant Brenda gives is [š]. It is interesting that here, as in the case of the [tʰ]/[kʰ] variation mentioned above, when Brenda does not have the necessary contrast in her system to reflect the adult contrast, what she changes is the point of articulation. In the case of adult [č], she retains the feature [−continuant] and varies on either side of the point of articulation. In the case of adult [f], she uses her one fricative [š], even though it has a different point of articulation, that is, she retains the feature [+continuant].

The fricative [ð] occurs only once. It should be noted that in her parents' speech [ð] varies with [d]. This variation is along an English: Hawaiian-English scale.

III.7.4   Glides, [w], [y], [r], [h], and [ʔ] in BRENDA II, Tape (071)

[w] and [y] are quite rare in this session. [w], however, seems to be quite well established. It is used in two words, *wowow* (Brenda's word for *dog*) and *walk*. [y] on the other hand only occurs twice, in [peyɛ] *pen* and [yutʰu] *you too*.

Just what the status of [r] might be is hard to say. In most cases it is probably best to consider this symbol to represent retroflexion of a vowel as in [brɛndə]. However, in one spontaneous instance only, *Ralph*, it represents a consonantal segment. It also occurs in the imitated *write*. In position where Brenda's parents have a final [r] in variation with [∅] Brenda in (071) has no final [r]. However, [ʔ], [o], and [u] are found in that position, e.g. [gɔdəʔ] *corder* ("tape recorder"), [tʰekʰo] *Checkers*, and [bæu] *bear*.

[h] is found in initial position with one exception—one case it varied with [ʔ] in final position.

Determination of the status of the glottal stop [ʔ] is quite difficult. It is found to vary with [p] (e.g. [tʰeipči] ~ [tʰeiʔči] *tape*) and with [∅] (e.g. [mami] ~ [mamiʔ] *mommy*). It also is found in places where the adult has [t] (e.g. *cut, hat*), [r] (e.g. *corder*), and [∅] (e.g. [šiʔ] *see*). In the cases where the glottal stop varies with another stop, it appears to be Brenda's first or most natural attempt at the adult stop. However, in the cases where the adult language has no stop and yet Brenda has [ʔ], do we want to say that it is her "word boundary"? The later discussion of intonation may make this somewhat clearer (IV.3). What may be the most plausible explanation is that Brenda is attempting to control the length of voicing. To do this she uses a glottal closure rather than a more gradual relaxation of voicing. In that case it would, in fact, represent a word boundary on the surface but which in some cases is neutralized with zero.

III.7.5   Vowels in BRENDA II, Tape (071)

If the consonants are unclear in many respects, the vowels are even less clear. It seems as if Brenda uses the following vowels systematically: [i], [ɪ], [e], [ɛ], [æ], [a], [u], and [o]. She also has the diphthongs [ei], [əi], and [əu]. The front/back distinction is quite clear. We have [šiʔ] for *horsie* and [šu] (or [šuʔ]) for *shoe*. Other distinctions are not as clear. Particularly there is the problem of vowel height in the front vowels. In one case, 284 through 294, Brenda says *daddy* eleven times. It varies from [didiʔ], which occurs once, to [dædi], which occurs five times. [dedi] also occurs five times. On the basis of this case, we would want to say that there was no contrast. However, in most other cases the vowel height seems to be more consistent.

Here, as in the phonology discussed earlier, the solution lies in saying that only a broad distinction can be claimed, but within that broader distinction Brenda approximates what will later become narrower distinctions. In that case, we would say Brenda has at this time a contrast between front and back vowels and a three-way distinction in height—that is, the basic five vowel system *a*, *e*, *i*, *o*, and *u*.

III.7.6   Utterances Not Included in This Description

The data that have been considered here represent about forty-five percent of the total utterances found on the tape. It should be remembered from Table 3 that around fifty-five percent of the utterances were unintelligible. Because of the impossibility of determining the meaning of these other utterances, we cannot know to what extent they are still within Brenda's phonological system. However, we can say that this fifty-five percent is highly regular in phonetic shape. Much of this percentage is made up of utterances of the sort mentioned above (III.6.1); that is, not full words but those utterances leading up to an intelligible word. We can see in retrospect that although these are not to be considered words themselves, they are in some way part of the production of the words under study.

Among the remaining utterances, there are a few segments and one cluster that are not found elsewhere: [z], [ž], [dz], [ndz], [mb], [x], [tʷ], and the cluster [ŋd]. However, these each occur only once, and because of their rarity it does not seem plausible that they form part of any regular system. On the whole, the utterances of the fifty-five percent unintelligible data do not go outside the system outlined above for the intelligible utterances. This gives reason to believe that, although based on a small portion of Brenda's total output, it is at least fairly representative of her system.

III.7.7 Summary of the First Session (071) BRENDA II

This study will always remain incomplete because of the inaccessibility of further data for testing hypotheses. However, we can say in general that the stops, including nasals, show quite a similarity to the adult system. Also, we have seen the beginnings of word-final consonants. Notice that those finals of the adult system that are used by Brenda are the final segments that correspond to the best-established initial segments in her own system. These changes in Brenda's system indicate considerable development over the final system of BRENDA I.

III.8 BRENDA II, Eighth Session (141) Age 1;8.21

In session eight (141) eight weeks later, Brenda used 71 words (types). They can be broken into the same four categories as before:

(1) 32 spontaneous words that had been used in more than one session.

(2) 27 spontaneous words that occur in only this session.

(3) 2 modeled words that occurred previously. (Note that one of these, *Suzie*, was only modeled previously—it never occurred spontaneously.)

(4) 10 words that were modeled in this session only.

It should be mentioned that these four groups represent around eighty-five percent of Brenda's total output—a much higher degree of intelligibility than in the first session (071) of BRENDA II.

III.8.1 Spontaneous Compared with Modeled Words

In Table 5, a list is given of the words of (141). Both a spontaneous form and a modeled form are given in some cases. It is

TABLE 5. The Words of (141)

Gloss	Spontaneous Form	Modeled Form
I. Spontaneous—used in more than one session		
1. black	bwæk^h	bwæk
2. Brenda	brɛndə	brɛndə
3. car	k^{h}a	—
4. carry	k^{h}æwri	k^{h}æwi (k^{h}e:i)
5. Charlotte	halɛt	—
6. circle	šıko	—
7. cook	k^{h}uk^h	k^{h}uk^h
8. finger	p^{h}iŋgə	—
9. fly	fwai	—
10. flying	faiĩŋ	fawĩ (faiĩŋ)
11. good	gut (gu^ʔ)	—
12. got	ga^ʔ	—
13. hiding	haidi:	haidĩŋ (haidĩ)
14. hurt	hərt	—
15. lantern	yæntın (wã̈tən)	—
16. man	mæn	—
17. milk	mıwk	—
18. mine	main	—
19. mommy	mami	—
20. my turn	mait^{h}un	—
21. no	nəo	—
22. Ron	ran	—
23. share	šæ^ʔ	—
24. step	tɛp$^{(h)}$	tɛ^ʔ (tɛp^h)
25. stuck	t^{y}ʌk$^{(h)}$	—
26. tape	t^{h}eip	—
27. there	dɛə	dɛə
28. toe	t^{h}ou	—
29. turn	t^{h}un	t^{h}ən
30. walk	wak	—
31. walking	wakĩŋ (wakĩ^ʔ)	—
32. window	wındo	wındo
II. Spontaneous—not occurring in another session		
1. balloon	brũ	bwũ/bwun
2. boy	boi	bəi (boi)
3. button	bət^{h}ın	bət^{h}ın
4. ca (mera)	kæ	—

TABLE 5—*Continued*

Gloss	Spontaneous Form	Modeled Form
5. give	(giɛuf, giɛv) gɪv	—
6. head	hɛtʰ	hɛ
7. itai	ɪtʰai	—
8. I went	əwɛu	—
9. lost	(rɔš) rwɔs	—
10. now	nau	—
11. oops	əps	—
12. owl(s)	aw(š)	awu
13. page	peč	—
14. Peter	pʰido	pʰido (pʰidɛ)
15. pink	pʰĩʔ	—
16. pink car	(pʰĩʔa) pʰĩʔkʰa	—
17. pixie	pʰiks (pʰič)	—
18. please	pʰiš	—
19. pop	pʰapʰ	—
20. read	ritʰ	—
21. rolling	(roĩŋ) rowĩŋ	—
22. say	šæ	—
23. self	šæuf	—
24. something	səmtʰɛ	—
25. touch	tʰəč	—
26. triangle	taiŋgo/træŋgo	jræŋgo (čægo)/ tɛŋgo, tæŋgo
27. went	wɛnt, yɛʔn, rɛnt	

III. Modeled but in more than one session
1. juice		duši
2. Suzie (only modeled previously)		šuši ʔ

IV. Modeled just this session
1. bump		bəmp/ bəm(ʔ)
2. can		kæn
3. curtain		kutʰɪn
4. find		faind (fain)
5. going		guin
6. microphone		məikrɔ̃ʔɔ̃/məikʸu
7. mike		məiʔ
8. nighttime		naitaim
9. pumpkin		pʰəmpʰɛn/pʰəmpʰɛʔ
10. witch		wɛč

frequently the case that after Brenda says a word some other speaker will repeat it. Brenda will then say the word again. In some of these cases (but not all) there is a marked difference between the form as Brenda says it spontaneously and the form when she has a model. An example is the word *hiding*. The full sequence is as follows:

(141)2   haidi:

                 (R)   Hide? What's hiding?

  3   brũ:

                     Oh, the balloon? Where?
                     Where is it? Where is it?

  4   haidĩŋ

                     Where?

  5   haidĩ

                     The balloon?

  6   haidih
  7   haidi:
  8   haidi:
  9   haidʸi:

Brenda says *hiding* spontaneously as [haidi:]. After I model the word she adds the final [ŋ], i.e., [haidĩŋ]. Notice then that in successive repetitions her form finally predominates again, i.e., [haidi:]. For this reason a form was taken to represent the spontaneous form if there was no adult model within the previous five minutes. This type of change will be taken up again in more detail later in the discussion of imitation (Chapter 5).

III.8.2   The Effect of Construction on Phonology

In 121 through 123 Brenda says *head* [hɛtʰ]. I then say, "Poor Brenda. Poor Brenda bumped her head. It hurt?" She then says *bump.head.*, i.e., [bəmp.hɛ]. The question then is why does Brenda delete the final consonant in *head*. At this session, Brenda normally has a devoiced consonant in this position. It seems that because of the increased complexity of trying to make the longer imitation, that is, of the words *bumped her head*, the phonological complexity of what she says must be reduced.

One further example that may also be of this type can be seen in 158 and 159. Brenda says, *read.page.*([ritʰ.pec]). As will be seen in the discussion of stops for session (141), Brenda always contrasts [b] and [pʰ] in initial position. It is difficult to explain why in this case the aspiration is deleted unless, again, because of the higher complexity of this attempt at a two-word construction (vertical construction) the phonological contrast is not maintained. (See VII.1, where this point is discussed again.)

These examples are mentioned here to demonstrate that a discussion of phonology even at this quite rudimentary level cannot be isolated from other elements of the theory. This interaction between phonology and construction is significant, not only for construction but for phonology.

III.8.3   Stops in BRENDA II, Tape (141)

Since the stops were already fairly well developed in (071), not too much change is evident here. The several inconsistencies in (071) have virtually disappeared. With three exceptions, voiceless stops are aspirated. One of these has been mentioned in III.8.2 as being affected by the longer construction within which it occurs. A second *ca(mera)*, that is, [kæ] is unexplained. The third exception will be discussed under clusters. Otherwise, stops maintain a three-way distinction for point of articulation: labial, alveolar, and velar; and a two-way distinction between voiced on the one hand and aspirated on the other in all positions except final position. As in (071) all final stops are voiceless, with the aspirated and nonaspirated forms in free variation.

III.8.4   Nasals in BRENDA II, Tape (141)

Nasals are much the same as in the adult system. There are several interesting occasions in which [ŋ] in the final position (*-ing*) is either deleted or replaced by the glottal stop [ʔ]. In both cases, the preceding vowel is nasalized. In one case where the adult has [ŋk], that is, *pink*, Brenda has [pʰĩʔ].

III.8.5   Fricatives and Affricates in BRENDA II, Tape (141)

Brenda used the fricatives [š], [h], [f], and, once, [v]. She used the affricates [č] and [ǰ]. The places in which they are used are interesting in reference to the adult system. In the first place, there is no voicing contrast in final position except in the one case of the word *give*. Brenda says:

(141)108   giɛuf
    109   giɛv
    110   giv

That is, with persistence in one case she succeeded in making the voicing distinction in final position.

In initial position, Brenda used [š] in words such as *self*, *something*, and *say*. In the word *Charlotte*, however, she uses [h]— [halɛt]. In other cases, for example *hiding*, she uses [h] where expected. [f] is used where it is normally found in adult English; however, in one instance she replaces it with [pʰ], that is, *finger*. It is interesting to note that this is in the case of a vertical construction, *finger.touch*. (See VII.3 for definitions of types of vertical construction.)

In final position [š] varies with [s] where the adult has the cluster [st]. [š] is used where the adult has [z], for example *owls* and *please*.

The only occurrence of [ǰ] is in variation with [č] in the word *triangle* and this only in imitation of an adult. Otherwise [d] is found in places where the adult has [j], for example [duši] *juice*. [č] is found word-final in *page* as well as in place of [ks] in *pixie*.

In general, then, it can be said that since (071) Brenda has added [f] and [č] to her system. It is interesting that in (071) we saw an example of [tʰ] and [kʰ] varying where one would expect [č]. That is, she was maintaining the feature [−continuant] and varying the point of articulation. Now, in the case of the cluster [ks] she uses her one affricate [č], which happens to be at the point of articulation between the two elements of the cluster.

III.8.6   Liquids and Glides in BRENDA II, Tape (141)

Liquids and glides are the least fully developed of the consonants in (141). In initial position, there is no contrast between [r] and [l], for example *lost* [rwɔs], *read* [ritʰ]. In one case, the initial [l] is replaced first by [w] and then by [y] in the word *lantern*.

In medial position, the glide [w] replaces both [l] and [r], for example *rolling* [roĩŋ] ~ [rowĩŋ] and *carry* [kʰæri]. The symbol [wr] represents in this case a segment neither clearly liquid nor glide. Notice in the case of *rolling* that the first attempt has nothing in the place of the medial liquid, and the second attempt includes [w]. This seems to be an indication of some natural restriction on production that with repeated effort Brenda can lift to some extent.

The liquid [l] when it appears before another consonant as in *self*, *milk*, or in the case of the syllabic [l] in *triangle*, is replaced by the vowel [u] or [o]. (The status of the liquids in this position is difficult to determine because of variation in the parents' speech on a Standard English : Hawaiian-English scale in the case of the father and a Standard English : Japanese-English scale in the case of the mother.) In the case of [r], the syllabic [r̩] as in *Peter* becomes [o], that is, [pʰido]. When [r] precedes another consonant, there is variation. In *lantern* we find [yæntin], but *turn* is rendered as [tʰun]. *Hurt* is [hərt].

One glide, [w], is well established in positions where it is expected from the adult system. However, because of its use in Brenda's system in places where the adult has the liquids *l* and *r*, its status in Brenda's system considered independently of the adult system is difficult to determine.

III.8.7   Clusters in BRENDA II, Tape (141)

Clusters with liquids have been mentioned above when the liquid precedes the other consonant. There are a number of cases of consonants followed by liquids. The most common is [br], which, perhaps because it appears so frequently in Brenda's name, is very well established. The cluster [bʷ] appears in *black* and in *balloon* in imitation. [pl] does not occur. In the word *please* we find [pʰ]. *Fly* is pronounced with either [fʷ] or [f]. The clusters [ps] and [ks] both occur as the only examples of clusters that correspond exactly to adult clusters in the words *oops* and *pixie*, respectively.

One exception referred to in the discussion of stops (III.8.3) has been left until now since it is part of an interesting set of contrasts when compared with the adult system. It is somewhat commonplace to say that the child will represent the adult [tʰ] as [tʰ] and the adult [st] as [t]. In this session Brenda was kind enough to say *tape. step*. [tʰei.tɛʔ] and give us a real example of this contrast. *Toe*, *touch*, and *turn* all have initial [tʰ] which indicates control over this segment. However, for *stuck* she gives [tʸʌk] on one occasion and [tʰʌkʰ] on another. That is to say, Brenda appears to be making a further distinction. She seems to be making a three-way contrast between [tʰ], [t], and [tʸ]. If phonetic conditioning were taken to be the explanation, one would not expect [ʌ] to cause palatalization in [tʸʌk] while [ə] in *touch* [tʰəč] does not.

This contrast will be returned to in the discussion of the intervening sessions. For now, it is better to focus on a second phenomenon. In the word *lost* we see [rəš] and [rwɔs]. That is to say, in final position it is not the case at all that adult [st] is replaced by [t]. It is replaced rather by [š] ~ [s]. It should be pointed out that in the parents' speech [st] ~ [s] in final position.

III.8.8 Vowels in Brenda II, Tape (141)

Since this does not pretend to be a full phonological analysis of (141), it will be sufficient to say that the vowels by this stage of Brenda's development are very much like the vowels in the adult system. There is an additional source of vowels in Brenda's system in those places where vowels are altered to represent liquids in the adult system. We have already seen what may be examples of this, such as in *turn* [tʰun] and *Peter* [pʰido]. Again, it must be noted that while these developments have been observed for the acquisition of Standard English (e.g. Edwards, 1973), similar processes are occurring in variation between Standard English and Hawaiian English.

III.8.9 Conclusion to BRENDA II, Eighth Session (141)

As this study has progressed and Brenda's linguistic ability has developed, the inadequacy of the half-hour session becomes more apparent. With a vocabulary the size of Brenda's it becomes more difficult to be sure that what occurs spontaneously in one-half hour represents the full extent of her system. It is for this reason, plus the fact that this study is not primarily a study of phonology, that this section on phonology has been restricted to these quite general notes and examples. We can see, however, that Brenda's system has developed to a point of high intelligibility to adults. Vowels, stops, nasals, the fricatives [š], [h], and [f] are very similar to those in the adult system. The liquids and affricates remain to be developed. The liquids at this stage have only begun to appear in initial position. In other positions they show up in their effect on the vowels.

III.9 Intervening Sessions (081–131), Ages 1;7.9 to 1;8.17

Since the data of (141) have been somewhat inconclusive, it will help to look back at several things that appear in the earlier sessions. First, we can look further into the problem of the reduction of initial clusters.

Table 6 gives nine words that appear throughout the eight sessions. Notice that the word *tape* always has [tʰ] except in (121)

TABLE 6. Development of Some Stops in BRENDA II

Word	Session							
	071	081	091	101	111	121	131	141
tape	tʰ	tʰ	tʰ	—	tʰ	{ tʰ / tʸ / t }	—	tʰ
tall	—	—	tʰ	—	—	t	—	—
talk	—	—	{ tʰ / tʸ }	—	{ tʰ / t }	—	—	—
tickle	—	tʰ	{ tʰ / č }	—	—	—	—	—
toe	—	tʰ	—	—	—	tʰ	—	tʰ
turn	—	tʰ	tʰ	—	—	—	—	tʰ
two	—	{ t / tʸ }	—	—	{ tʰ / tʸ }	tʸ	{ tʸ / ǰ }	—
step	—	—	—	{ tʰ / č }	—	—	t⁽ʰ⁾	tʸ
stuck	—	—	—	tʰ	t	{ tʰ / č / t }	—	tʸ

where [tʰ], [tʸ], and [t] all occur. For that same session *tall* occurs without aspiration, *toe* with aspiration. The initial of *two* is the palatalized [tʸ]. The palatalization of the stop in *two* is not problematic because of the following vowel. (Note: [t] varies with [tʸ] in (081), [tʰ] with [tʸ] in (111), and [tʸ] with [ǰ] in (131)). But in this session (121) *stuck* has [tʰ], [č], and [t] as the initial consonant. That is to say, it is only in the last session (141) that the three-way contrast suggested in III.8.7 between [tʰ], [t], and [tʸ] occurs.

In the development of the word *step* we can see some of the same alternation. First we see in (101) that [tʰ] varies with [č]. In the next session in which it occurs (131), it occurs both aspirated and unaspirated. It is only in (141) that it occurs only unaspirated.

In summary of Table 6, we can see that this contrast between aspirated and unaspirated stops in the child's system to represent aspirated stops and a cluster respectively in the adult's system is not clear at any stage of BRENDA II. By tape (141), it seems to have reached a certain amount of stability, but it is apparently still in the process of development.

A second thing that can be seen by a look at the earlier data is several instances of word-final voiced consonants. In (141) it was said that this contrast did not exist; yet one week earlier *bug* and *big* occurred with voiced finals. Two weeks earlier *good* appeared as [gudu].

In general these isolated pieces of data give evidence that it is virtually impossible to consider the child's developing system either whole or entirely consistent at any one time. What we see instead is a generally valid consistency with notable exceptions.

Finally, one rather difficult sequence from (091) should be considered. Brenda is drawing pictures with Charlotte. Charlotte draws a picture of a girl with long legs and large polka dots on her dress. First Brenda says *tall* [tʰə] three times, then *Brenda*. She then stands up and stretches up on her tiptoes and says *tall clown*. But it was not as direct as that. What she really said is this:

(091) 81 tʰɔ
      82 tʰə
      83 tʰæʔ
      84 kʰæʔ
      85 kʰəãũ
      86 kʰɔ̃ãũ

Utterance 81 is clearly *tall* on the basis of her phonology at that time and on the basis of other production of the word with which this was identical. The form of 81 [tʰɔ] would also be an acceptable pronunciation in adult Hawaiian English. Utterance 86 was clearly *clown* on the basis of her other productions of that word. What were 82 through 85? It appears that Brenda has a mental representation of both words, but for some reason when they are in sequence one interferes with the other. She seems to go from *tall* to *clown* by a succession of alterations of one element at a time. She changes the vowel, adds the glottal stop, assimilates the [tʰ] to the glottal stop, and then changes the vowel and drops the glottal stop when she nasalizes the final vowels. Hockett (1967) has called words of this type in adult speech "blends." He points to their importance as a means of elucidating general design features of language. Hockett feels that it is "possible to think of a language as a system whose design is reflected not only by the utterances produced by its speakers but also by the process of production itself" (p. 911). In this case it certainly appears that one word is in some way interfering with the other, and I feel that it is inadequate to describe this as simply a "performance error." That is, I agree with Hockett that we can learn something about what language is by seeing how it works. In this case it looks as if these words are in a vertical construction (i.e., *tall.clown.*) that causes the phonetic confusion (see VII.3). There is an interaction between constructional complexity and phonological complexity so that words that are easily pronounced separately become somewhat more difficult in construction.

III.10   Conclusion to Phonology Study

We have seen several examples of Brenda's successive improvement of a word. For example, in (071) there was the case of *shoe* being carefully worked on in whisper before a loud attempt was made. In (141) we saw the case of *give* [giɛuf.giɛv.giv] where in three successive attempts the word gets closer to the adult surface form. This represents the case where Brenda is apparently aware of some target form and can actually improve her production with practice and without further help from others.

On the other hand, we have seen cases where although Brenda's spontaneous form is intelligible to adults, it improves when she has a model. An example of this improvement is *hiding* from (141) above (III.8.1). With a model it is [haidĩŋ], but then as she repeats it drifts back to her original form, first [haidĩ] and then [haidi:]. This is evidence for the opposite process to that just mentioned above. That is, when Brenda has an immediate model she can produce a form closer to the adult form, but as the memory wanes apparently so does the ability to produce. These two processes seem to establish a central level of production that represents Brenda's target surface form. With repetition she can improve it and with imitation improve it considerably more.

There is good evidence that Brenda can remember forms well beyond her ability to produce them. An example is that of *microphone* which I rehearsed with her in tape (141). She was able to say [məikrɔ̃ˀɔ̃], [məikʸu], and [məikʸo] only after my careful (and this one time insistent) pronunciation. Two months later, she said [məikʸəfon] quite spontaneously as I got out my tape recorder and microphone.

There is evidence, then, for three types of words: (1) words that are used spontaneously with relatively little variation, (2) words that are built up over a string of false starts, and (3) words that are imitated and show phonological characteristics in advance of the current spontaneous system. Words of the first type are, perhaps, the best indicators of Brenda's basic system at any particular time. Words of the second and third types have forms that are altered on the basis of their context. This context may be an immediate model by another speaker, a string of rehearsals by Brenda, or the position of the word in a construction of larger complexity. This sensitivity to context at several levels indicates the interaction of Brenda's phonological system with her ability to construct or, as will be discussed later, her ability to carry on a conversation.

CHAPTER IV

Intonation

IV.1 Why Make a Special Study of Intonation?

Bever, Fodor, and Weksel (1965, 1971, p. 275) have stated that "it is widely accepted in the literature that the child effectively masters the intonation pattern of his language *before he has learned any words at all*." Miller and Ervin (1964, 1971) have noticed the use of stress to mark a distinction between a locative construction (e.g. *baby róom.*) and a possessive construction (e.g. *báby book.*). Brown and Bellugi-Klima (1964, 1971) have pointed out that it is on the basis of primary stress and terminal intonation contour that utterances are separated into sentences (horizontal constructions) and sequences of separate utterances (vertical constructions). When I began this study I felt it would be interesting to look for any development of the child's ability to control prosodic features in the period before sentence construction.

IV.1.1 Transcription of Intonation

As I mentioned before (II.2.2.3), the first transcriptions of intonation in Brenda's speech were made in musical notation. After a time, a set of more or less regular patterns began to emerge and this notation became unwieldy. I noticed that all of the utterances fell into four basic groups. The first, to which I assigned the symbol "F" was characterized by a falling intonation. These utterances began on a pitch and then fell a distance of at least a minor third—usually more than that. A second group, L, were level. Although there was a certain amount of variation in pitch, it was very small, and there was rarely any difficulty in distinguishing those that dropped slightly from those that dropped enough to be classed as falling (F). A third category, R, rose in pitch—again noticeably, that is, more than a minor third. A fourth category, C, represented all the rest, which showed a complex contour that was not a simple movement in one direction.

A second level of transcription of intonation was added, although later it did not seem to have any particular importance. The original four symbols, F, L, R, and C, were altered to FL, LL, RL, and CL to indicate an unusual length (L). I found, however, that since length was already being marked on the vowels in the transcription, this marking was really redundant and added nothing important.

After two sessions of transcription with the eight symbols (F, FL, L, LL, R, RL, C, CL), another interesting thing was noticed. In the F group, there appeared to be really two quite different types. The first of these as described above fell from some pitch to some other pitch at least a minor third below. In the second type, the fall was a longer fall and no final pitch could be determined; that is, the pitch and volume fell away at the same time. These were then transcribed FX—the X representing an "x" placed on the musical staff to indicate that no definite final pitch could be determined. Since the earlier tapes had not included this distinction, I had to retranscribe all of the F's to determine the extent of this special type.

IV.1.2   A Statistical Summary of Intonation Types in BRENDA I, Age 1;0.2 to 1;1.22

In Table 7 all of the utterances of BRENDA I are summarized by intonation type. Since there was a steady increase in the number of utterances from session to session, the raw figures have been given; below these figures the percentages for each type are given. It should be understood that no attempt has been made to perform any statistical operations on these figures. It is not suggested that they may or may not be statistically significant. They are presented here as the clearest way to represent the growth of one particular class of intonation type.

TABLE 7. Summary of Intonation in BRENDA I

Intonation Symbol	Session								Total
	012	021	022	031	032	041	042	051	
F	19	6	18	20	9	13	11	38	134
FX	11	1	16	37	78	27	71	102	343
L	22	4	29	23	55	74	14	33	254
R	6	5	1	4	4	13	6	5	44
C	8	12	10	30	7	17	7	5	95
(Misc.)[a]						(64)			(64)
Totals	66	28	74	114	153	207	109	183	934
F percent of Total	40.9	25.8	45.9	48.2	52.3	19.3	75.2	76.1	55.1
L percent of Total	25.8	10.7	39.2	17.5	35.9	35.7	14.6	18.1	27.2
F + L percent of Total	66.7	36.5	85.1	65.7	88.2	55.0	88.2	94.5	78.3
FX percent of Total	16.7	3.5	21.6	32.5	47.7	13.0	66.1	55.7	36.7
FX percent of F	40.8	14.3	47.1	67.3	89.0	67.5	87.7	72.9	71.9

[a]Some of these may have, in fact, been in the other categories. They were not transcribed since their status as separate utterances is somewhat questionable.

The percentages are listed by the following five groups:

(1) F percent of the total. This figure represents all F's including the special FX type.

(2) L percent of the total.

(3) F + L percent of the total.

(4) FX percent of the total. The purpose of this percentage is to show the relative importance of this group in the whole corpus.

(5) FX percent of the F group. This figure shows the growing place of this special type within all the F group.

If we look at the percentages listed for each of these five groups, an interesting development shows up. First, in looking at (1) F percent of total, we can see that this falling contour, although important in the earliest sessions, grows by (051) to more than three-fourths of the total utterances. Notice the decreases in (021) and (041). In (021) Brenda was sick and was not responsive in general. Her most typical utterance that session was a long string of velar nasals interspersed with whining. Notice also the low total number of utterances. Session (041) is unusual in a number of ways. There were quite a few (64 altogether) utterances that were difficult to transcribe. They were mostly nasalized schwa [ə̃] and occurred just before other utterances. It was difficult to decide just how to treat these. Since they did not show up in the next session, they were left in abeyance as something so far inexplicable.

The second group (2) grows somewhat at first and then decreases in importance. However, the third group (3) shows that between the two types F and L most of the distribution is taken up—94.5 percent of the total in (051). It is clear that these two groups will include most of Brenda's speech at this time.

The fourth and fifth groups (4) and (5) show that the FX type of utterance has grown to be more than half the total of Brenda's utterances and that among the falling (F) types most of those are FX.

IV.1.3   Primary Stress and Terminal Contour

It should be clear that the intonation type that I have transcribed as FX corresponds exactly to English primary stress and terminal contour. This set of statistics has provided an interesting fact. From these data it can be seen that primary stress and terminal contour are the products of development. Lieberman (1967) and Painter (1971) have claimed that this FX is the natural product of the process of vocalization. To activate the vocal chords the subglottal pressure rises, vocalization takes place, and then as the subglottal pressure drops off the pitch falls and the volume falls to nothing. This quite accurately describes the FX intonation contour. What remains to be explained is why this process develops over time if it is a natural process of vocalization. Shouldn't we expect this contour to be found first and then later to find levels, rises, and so on? It is true that in the first session there were falling pitches present in large enough number to indicate some preference for this type. What seems most plausible is that in the early stages Brenda's control over voicing and subglottal pressure is incomplete. The result of this incomplete control is that in some cases she actually overextends the period of subglottal pressure, which results in level intonation. Geoffrey Nathan (personal communication, December 1973) has suggested that intonation contours are, in fact, controlled before this period but that the complexity of developments in phonology result in a regression of intonation to an earlier stage. I think that this is undoubtedly the correct explanation but a clear description will have to await studies of children at even earlier stages of vocalization than this.

A question raised by the variation between F and L contours is whether there is any predictability about falling (F) and level (L) on the basis of syllable structure or context. Table 8 gives a list of Brenda's eight words in session (051) along with the intonation contours for each. Notice that with one exception Brenda's words at this time are characterized by FX or F. That is to say, when she says a word that is recognizable, she gives it primary stress and terminal contour. The one exception is interesting. The word *e* is pronounced level nine out of ten times. This word may be recognized as equivalent to the Japanese *e*, that is *yes*. This is one of the few words of Japanese the mother uses regularly with Brenda, and it is not surprising that it has become part of Brenda's speech. What is interesting in this context is that this word is not treated by Brenda in the same way as the others. It does not receive the same stress and intonation. These results seem to indicate that Brenda has learned English primary stress by (051) and also learned that it is English and where not to apply it. Of course, this is an important claim and should be investigated with further studies of truly bilingual children.

TABLE 8. Intonation for the Eight Words Session (051)

	FX	*F*	*L*	*C*	*R*	*Total*
1. awəu	26	14	7	2	0	49
2. nau	22	2	3	1	1	29
3. dædi	14	6	2	0	0	22
4. dæyu	8	5	2	0	1	16
5. nene	8	4	2	0	0	14
6. e	1	0	9	0	0	10
7. mæmə	5	1	0	1	0	7
8. ada	6	0	0	0	0	6
Unclassified	13	4	9	1	3	30
						183

Having said this much about the two categories F and FX, it is fair to ask if any distinction can be found to exist between these two types. As far as I can determine from the data of (051), there is, in fact, no distinction in use between these two types. It should be noted here that for the Hawaiian English of Brenda's father the question intonation, at least for direct questions with *yes/no* answers, is a fall from a high pitch to a lower pitch. Vanderslice and Pierson (1967) give a full discussion of this intonation. For example, they give (p. 162) *you brought milk?* in which *you* is high pitch, *brought* at a still higher pitch, and *milk* has the lowest pitch. In a longer question, the high pitch is maintained throughout with a low pitch only on the final syllable. For Brenda's parents, particularly the father, this question intonation varies with the Standard English rising intonation. In (051) there is no evidence that either the F or the R are used for questions by Brenda. A large number of Brenda's utterances are responses to the mother's (or my) questions, and so the most appropriate response is the declarative intonation.

IV.1.4 Stress in Bisyllabic Words

In the discussion above, no distinction has been made between monosyllabic words and bisyllabic words. It could be questioned whether or not there is any systematic placement of stress on one or the other of the syllables in words of two syllables. The list below gives some examples.

(051)6   néne
    9   nené
   28   ǽwǝu
   29   awǝ́u

   47   dedí
   48   dædí
   49   dǽdí
   50   dǽdi
   51   dedí
   52   dǽdi

  172   áwǝ
  173   awǝ́

As can be seen from these few examples, there appears to be no regularity in the placement of stress. It might be suggested that there is a relationship between stress and vowel quality from examples 28 and 29 above, with [æ] receiving stress. However, the following examples indicate that this is not the case.

(051)53   ála
     54   ælǝ́

The repetition of the same word ⟨dædi⟩ but with different stress rules out a differential application of stress based on semantic intent.

IV.1.5   Developments after (051) in BRENDA I

The data given above have covered the period from (012) age 1;0.2 (051) 1;1.22 because in many ways this period is more homogeneous than if it were to be extended to (061) or (S11). As I showed in the discussion of phonology, Brenda's system by (051) was already in the process of change. In the later several tapes, the change becomes considerable. The list below gives the intonation figures for (S11), which is four weeks after (051).

(1) F percent of total   50.5
(2) L percent of total   33.1
(3) F + L percent of total   83.6
(4) FX percent of total   15.6
(5) FX percent of F   29.4

Notice that the category FX shows a decrease within F as well as F showing an overall decrease. The level (L) group has increased in importance. There is also one new minor development. Some of these utterances (seven out of 275) fell, then rose slightly as the pitch was released. These two developments are indications that Brenda was actively trying to control the final timing of the release with the dropping of subglottal pressure.

IV.1.6 Conclusion to BRENDA I Intonation

During the period of BRENDA I, Brenda has developed English primary stress and terminal contour up to a peak at (051). As her phonology begins to become elaborated, she enters a period in which she has to readjust her timing to account for new phonological conditions. Stress and intonation contour can be seen to develop to a certain extent independent of segmental phonology.

IV.2 Intonation Statistics for BRENDA II, Ages 1;7.2 to 1;8.21

As in the case of BRENDA I, I transcribed all the utterances of BRENDA II for intonation by use of the symbols described above (IV.1). Table 9 gives a summary of these figures for BRENDA II. It should be remembered that at the end of BRENDA I the category of F (falling) had become central in Brenda's system. I suggested that this represents the basic stress pattern of English. In light of that, it is interesting to notice that overall the F category has fallen in use (46.7 percent for the total period) and the L category has risen (42.2 percent for the total period). The sum of the two figures is still, however, very high—that is, 88.9 percent of the total of Brenda's output falls into these two categories. It is clear that the discussion of intonation in BRENDA II will have to explain these figures.

IV.3 Interpretation of Table 9

The first question that must be answered is: If the F category represents primary stress and final contour, why the emergence of the L category? The explanation may be related to the fact that during this period Brenda is in the process of acquiring word-final consonants. These final consonants have the effect of keeping the level of phonation up until the consonant produces the stop.

A look at the relation between the L contour and the phonetic

TABLE 9. Summary of Intonation in BRENDA II

Intonation Symbol	Session								Total
	071	081	091	101	111	121	131	141	
F (total)	130	111	131	165	306	171	196	162	1372
FX	38	28	55	50	109	77	69	40	466
L	174	159	174	242	196	90	84	123	1242
R	26	14	9	8	10	11	19	16	113
C	38	25	40	12	35	9	41	24	214
Totals	368	309	354	427	547	281	330	325	2940
F percent of Total	35.3	35.9	37.0	38.6	55.9	60.9	59.4	49.8	46.7
L percent of Total	47.3	51.5	49.2	56.7	35.8	32.0	25.5	37.8	42.2
F + L percent of Total	82.6	87.4	86.2	95.3	91.8	92.9	84.9	87.6	88.9
FX percent of Total	10.3	9.1	15.5	11.7	19.9	27.4	20.9	12.3	15.5

shape of words in BRENDA II confirms this hypothesis. The following four rules cover the large majority of cases found:

(1) Words of the shape CV are F (falling)
(2) Words of the shape CVCV are F (falling)
(3) Words of the shape CVC are L (level)
(4) Words of the shape CVN are L (level). (N represents any nasal segment.)

Both the F and the L intonation are in fact primary stress. What is distinguished is the effect of the final consonant. Notice the case of rules (3) and (4) above. There is apparently some similarity between the nasal stop [n] and voiceless stops. The word *Ron* occurred in (111) as [rãtʰ]. By (141) it was [ran].

IV.3.1   Development of Intonation by (141)

By the time of (141), Brenda had begun to gain control of the final consonants. For this session the four rules above have to be given with exceptions. (1) and (2) remain the same. (3) holds but with the exceptions of the words *hurt*, *milk*, *step*, *read*, and *give*. That is to say in some cases, but not all, Brenda is able to produce words of the shape CVC with primary stress and falling contour.

Rule (4) needs some elaboration. A distinction must be made between [n] and [m]. From early in BRENDA II, words ending in [m] were falling; that is, [m] was not equivalent to the group of voiceless stops. In places where [n] was expected on the basis of adult forms, Brenda treated it the same as a voiceless stop originally. By (141), however, she gave several words ending in [n] the F contour. In several cases (i.e., *Ron* and *turn*), there was no consistency—some instances being F and some L.

IV.3.2   Stress of Syllables

In BRENDA I, I pointed out that no significance could be ascribed to the placement of stress on either syllable of a bisyllabic word. By (071) this placement has become highly consistent. Stress is placed on the penultimate syllable. For example there are *báby*, *Brénda*, *dáddy*, *mómmy*, *mónster*, and *páper*. But also notice *hot wáter* [haʔwádə], which may be a trisyllabic word for Brenda (see VII.2 for discussion of this form). Also notice what may or may not be one word in (131)148 *no fáir*. There is only one regular exception to this general rule. In (131) Brenda inexplicably stresses the second syllable of *ready* [rɛdí] in about half of the instances in which she uses the word. The explanation for this may be that in children's games to which Brenda is frequently exposed, such as hide-and-seek, the searcher often announces the beginning of the search by calling out [rɛːdíː] (*ready?*). Otherwise, any placement of stress on the final syllable appears to be accidental.

A related phenomenon is Brenda's choice of syllable when her word is a reduced form of a longer adult word. For example, in (071) Brenda uses [šiʔ] for *horsie*. However, by the next week, in spite of the 14 tokens of [šiʔ] in (071), she has shifted to [haš]. This is apparently more consistent with what is a general practice of using the stressed syllable of the adult word as she does, for example, in *cucumber* [kʸukʰ]. A further consideration is that this form for *horsie* is homophonous with her form in (071) for *see* [šiʔ]. The shift to [haš], of course, eliminates the homophony.

The only word in the corpus in which the adult word has final stress (*balloon*) Brenda gives as [brũː]. In this case, she has kept the initial consonant and the final syllable.

IV.4   Prosodic Variation and Semantic Contrast

Brown (1973) raises the question of whether or not the variation in intonation patterns in the one-word period indicates semantic contrast. He quotes Bloom (1973) as saying that prosodic patterns do "not seem to be used for semantic contrast prior to the onset of syntax" (p. 153). He further reports the Menyuk and Bernholz (1969) research in which they have claimed the opposite results, that is, prosodic features have been used to indicate (1) statement, (2) question, and (3) emphasis. My data agree with Bloom's conclusion. Although there is considerable variation, most of it can be predicted on the basis of syllable structure and phonological content. There is apparently no semantic contrast. For example, there is the following sequence from (141)—the end of the one-word period.

```
(141)10   brɛndɛʔ   F
     11   brɛndə    FX
     12   brɛndəʔ   R
     13   brɛndə    F
     14   brɛndə    F
```

For these utterances, the context is unvarying, and yet there is an R within this group.

As another example look at this group from (141).

(141)	18	ran	F
	19	rən	L
	20	rən	C

Or:

(141)	40	brɛndu	L
	41	brɛndu	FX
	42	brɛndə	L

Or:

(141)	64	mami	FX
	65	mami	C
	66	mami	F

Or:

(141)	76	ran	F
	77	ran	R
	78	rən	L

Without even considering the question of what any one of these intonation contours might mean, it is clear, I think, that the variation in these repetitions within a set context reduces the possibility of contrast. It is for this reason that I have treated the development of intonation statistically rather than looking at separate occurrences of specific patterns. I feel that only the statistical observation of the prominence of the falling contour is justified from my study.

IV.5 Intonation and Speech Act Function

It might be suggested that intonation is performing speech act functions that may result in a different kind of contrastive use. Although the discussion of the speech acts themselves is presented in IX.3, that discussion is anticipated here in Table 10. This table lists the illocutionary acts performed in (051) at the end of BRENDA I, (071) at the beginning of BRENDA II, and (141) at the end of BRENDA II. The intonation contours observed for each illocutionary act are also given.

TABLE 10. Illocutionary Acts for Three Sessions

		F	L	R	C
	(051)				
II.a.1	Reference	20	1	—	1
2	Predication	20	1	1	—
II.b.1	Direct directive	21	3	—	—
4	Negative directive	2	2	—	—
	(071)				
II.a.1	Reference	21	47	3	3
2	Predication	8	15	2	1
5	Fictional	5	6	2	—
6	Imaginary	8	10	—	—
II.b.1	Direct directive	4	6	1	3
3	Self directive	7	4	2	1
II.c	Expressive	—	3	—	2
II.g	Handing	2	2	1	1
	(141)				
II.a.1	Reference	33	9	2	3
2	Predication	16	13	1	2
4	Assertion	—	2	—	—
5	Fictional	18	24	3	1
7	Negative, propositional	—	2	—	—
II.b.1	Direct directive	28	13	—	6
3	Self directive	19	6	2	1
4	Negative directive	—	1	—	—
II.d	Vocative	—	2	—	—
II.e	Commissive	—	1	—	—
II.f	Threat	4	2	—	—
II.g	Handing	3	1	—	—
II.h	Translative	3	—	—	—

As the figures in this table indicate, intonation is not being used to contrast illocutionary acts. In (051) and (141) there are more falling (F) than level (L) utterances and many more of falling and level than of rising and contour. This is true of the session taken as a whole as well as for specific illocutionary acts, which indicates a lack of contrast. The two exceptions to this general statement, II.b.3, Self directives in (071) and II.a.5 Fictional statements in

(141) do not appear to be significant. In session (071) the greater number of level (L) utterances reflects phonological conditions, that is, the development of word-final consonants.

IV.6   Conclusion to Intonation Study

By the end of BRENDA II, Brenda has learned that the basic stress in English is on the penultimate syllable. She has had to redevelop her control of terminal contour since the addition of final stops to her system had the effect of causing her to maintain level pitch. By (141), although Brenda's control of terminal contour is not complete, it is well on the way to becoming established. This calls into question the claim by Bever et al. (1965, 1971) that these prosodic features are controlled before learning any words. The solution is probably, as Nathan (personal communication) has suggested, that this apparent lack of control indicates an interaction in complexity between intonation and phonetic production. Since the terminal contour is one of the principal criteria by which other investigators such as Brown and Bellugi-Klima (1964, 1971) have been able to determine sentence construction, it is not surprising that control of this contour should be fairly well developed long before the process of sentence construction actually begins.

CHAPTER V
Discourse Redundancies

V.1 Imitation and Repetition

I have been postponing discussion of two important aspects of Brenda's speech, imitation and repetition. Earlier I said that the consideration of phonology and intonation was a relatively context-free aspect of this study. This must be qualified now since in presenting the material I was obliged to refer to context in several ways. In the first case, I had to use the context of an utterance as the only means of making a judgment to provide a translation or gloss. In discussing phonetic variation, I had to look at a sequence of utterances within a constant context as a means of making a judgment about sameness or difference. Finally, I had to separate imitation from spontaneous utterances as a means of getting at Brenda's productive system. This, of course, entailed a reference to the context to see if some other speaker had used the particular word under study.

I have now come to the place where these two concepts, imitation and repetition, can be seen to refer to two types of contexts of an utterance. In the first case, an imitated utterance is related to an earlier utterance of another speaker. In the second case, a repeated utterance is related to an earlier (immediately preceding) utterance of the same speaker, namely Brenda. Both are instances of the same general phenomenon of repetition. In this discussion, however, repetition will refer to the child's repetition of her own utterances. I have coined the term "discourse redundancies" to refer to imitation and repetition because they seem to function as a means of introducing redundancy within the context of discourse. In my use of "discourse" I am not making a distinction between "discourse" (the connected utterances of one speaker) and "dialogue" (the connected utterances of separate speakers). I am using "discourse" to mean a series of related utterances of either a single or several speakers (see VI.1).

V.1.1 Piaget's Play and Imitation

It is interesting to notice the similarity of the distinction between repetition and imitation in speech and that made by Jean Piaget in his treatment of play and imitation—or on the more general level, accommodation and assimilation. Piaget in many places, notably in his *Play, Dreams, and Imitation in Childhood* (1951), has argued that the process of cognitive development is a process of adaptation, the two poles of which represent the child's adaptation of his own structures to the world—accommodation— and the child's adaptation of the world to his own structures— assimilation.

In looking at Brenda's language development, we see that these two types of adaptation have clear manifestations even at this very early stage. In her imitation of adult words we will see to what extent her own system can be altered to match that of the adult. In her repetitions we will see what are the limits of the internal structures of her own system. It is from this point of view, then, that I will be looking at discourse redundancies.

V.2 Imitation—How Can One Tell?

The idea that children learn their language by imitation has been both championed and argued against for some time. One very basic methodological problem is rarely mentioned in these discussions: How can you tell if a child has imitated something? What are the limits of what will be accepted as imitation? Obviously if the adult says *doll* and the child says [da] it is easy to claim that it was imitated. However, if the child said [arwaөʌz], as Brenda did in tape (012), most likely everyone would agree that this was not an imitation of *doll*. But why? Clearly there is a tacit agreement that to be considered an imitation an utterance and its model must be within some undefined limits of similarity as judged by the investigator. Otherwise all utterances following adult utterances (i.e., all utterances) would have to be considered imitations. In that case, the argument that the child learns by imitation would be won a priori.

A second consideration is to determine somehow just what is being imitated. As in the case of [arawaɵʌz] above, if it was said with a particularly even intonation, it might perhaps be in imitation of the overall intonation contour of what the adult had said, even if every detail of the phonetic content were changed. In that case, it might have been a good imitation. Again, it is clear that some undefined assumptions are usually made about what is being imitated, and usually the model is taken to be the phonetic form.

From these points, it should be clear that when a child's utterance is taken to be an imitation, it is because it is within some area of overlap with the hearer's system. There is apparently some extension of one's own system that can be made, so that although [da] is not the phonetic shape of the word *doll* it can be understood as translating to that.

One final difficulty in studying imitation arises even if one accepts an undefined limit of intelligibility. The question is: How long can a child wait to imitate before the word falls into the group considered spontaneously produced? Is the latency two seconds, two minutes, two days? Bowerman (1973, p. 21) has defined imitations as follows: "A direct imitation was defined, as in the samples from Brown's subjects, as a complete or reduced rendition in the same word order, of another person's utterance which had occurred within the three utterances preceding the child's." That is, Bowerman along with Brown tends to think that the imitation should be more or less immediate to be called an imitation. Bowerman does not mention, however, over what time period those preceding three utterances may extend. The utterance cited in the chapter on phonology (III.4), (021)21 [čoda] is a good example of this problem. This word is problematic because there is no immediate instance of it in the input, so it is difficult to call it an imitation; yet it does not fit into what appears to be Brenda's productive system. An important consideration, then, in discussions of imitation is the latency of an imitation.

V.2.1 Spontaneous and Elicited Imitation

Table 11 lists a number of suspected imitations taken from each of the eight tapes (012) to (051). It is not unusual in these tapes of BRENDA I for the mother to prompt Brenda to say things. She is clearly trying to elicit imitations. The relative lack of success of this method is suggested by the items in Table 11. Out of the fifteen examples, eight (which are marked by an "E" following the example number) are elicited by an adult. The remaining seven utterances are spontaneous imitations (these are marked with "S").

Of the eight elicited imitations, all of them are cases of prompting by repeating a single word or stressing it in a slightly expanded version. For example, in E11 an adult says, "Dropped. Did it drop?" The spontaneous imitations are similar. Four are imitations of the last word said (E1, E7, E10, E14). In the other cases, the model is stressed. In E6 and E15 the model is stressed within a longer sentence. In E9 the phone is answered first by the father, then by the mother. The "hello" is given importance by position in initiating the phone conversation. The distinction between spontaneous and elicited imitations lies mainly in the other speakers' intentions, not in Brenda's response.

What is important, then, is not so much whether or not the imitation is elicited, but rather the position of the word, or the stress it receives, or both. Of course, in the elicited cases the adult's prompting takes the form of duplicating conditions under which the child imitates spontaneously.

Note that these examples are few compared with the total corpus, and particularly when compared with the number of times that prompting apparently failed. It should not be taken as an indication that this is in any way the most common or significant portion of the data.

Perhaps it would be useful now to review the terms that have been introduced. In the discussion of phonology, I made a distinction between a "modeled" utterance and a "spontaneous" utterance. A spontaneous utterance is one for which no model exists in the preceding recorded five minutes of the speech environment. "Modeled" is a neutral term that does not claim that the utterance is necessarily an imitation, but only that that possibility cannot be eliminated. It may or may not be an imitation. By an imitation I

Table 11. Imitation in BRENDA I

Example	Tape	Utterance	Time Lapse (Sec.)	Input Speech
E1 Ŝ[a]	(012)		$24\frac{1}{5}$	Kukla, Fran, and Ollie! x x x
	2	lei:		
E2 E	(012)		$23\frac{4}{5}$ $17\frac{4}{5}$	Doll x x x. Dada. Dada. x x x
	21	da		
	22	da		
E3 E	(012)		$9\frac{1}{5}$	Flower, hm? x x x
	30	flɔhə		
E4 E	(012)		$1\frac{2}{5}$	Hakata doll.
	10	ka		
E5 E	(021)		$19\frac{4}{5}$	Yellow. Yellow crayon. x x x
	1	iu:hU↑[b]		
E6 S	(021)		$23\frac{1}{5}$	What color do you like? x x x
	3	gæu		
E7 S	(021)		3	I got my farm books.
	8	bau		
E8 E	(022)		$10\frac{2}{5}$ 6	Boat? Boat?
	55	baæ		

[a] S indicates a spontaneous imitation. E indicates an elicited imitation.
[b] ↑ indicates ingressive airstream.

Tᴀʙʟᴇ 11—*Continued*

Example		Tape	Utterance	Time Lapse (Sec.)	Input Speech
E9	S	(031)		$14\frac{4}{5}$	Hello.
				$7\frac{2}{5}$	Hello.
		65	o		
E10	S	(032)			Can you read this book?
				9	
		21	bU?		
E11	E	(032)			Dropped. Did it drop?
				$4\frac{3}{5}$	
		152	dʌp		
E12	E	(041)		$8\frac{2}{5}$	Bears. Hm. Two bears.
				$9\frac{4}{5}$	
		24a	bə		
		24b	bæ		
E13	E	(041)			Telephone.
				4	
		191	tɛl		
E14	S	(042)			Where did it go? Where did it go?
				$14\frac{2}{5}$	
		55	geu		
E15	S	(051)121	ab		
		122	ada		
					She wants *another* one.
				$2\frac{3}{5}$	
		123	ada		
					Atha?
		124	adða?		
					Ada.

mean an utterance that can be clearly shown to be copied from another speaker. A "spontaneous imitation" is an utterance in which the child has not been specifically prompted for that word. An "elicited imitation" is one that has been specifically prompted. Unfortunately, these categories are easier to state quickly in this way than to determine in practice. For instance, what is the length of time prior to an utterance that should be considered? If someone in another room or on another day "models" a word, should it be classed as "modeled"? Or is it only "modeled" if it is in the same discourse within a short time? In this case, as in the case of the glosses, I have had to make judgments that ultimately go back to my own intuitions. The discussion that follows shows the approach I have taken with these problems.

V.2.2 Latency of Imitation

The question of latency was raised above. In Table 11, some time measurements are given to indicate the lapse between the model and the child's utterance. (I used a stop watch with $\frac{1}{5}$ second as the smallest interval. Of course, these measurements can be no more exact than my hearing and reflexes would allow.) In all cases but five (E2, E8, E9, E11 and E12), there was a single occurrence of the imitated word within a long period preceding the imitation. In those five cases where the word was repeated, time lapses are given for the repetitions.

Nothing too assertive should be said about these figures since the qualifications placed on the determination of imitations in the first place have suggested the tentative nature of this area of study. However, two things can be noticed. The first is that in the first session (012) there are several cases of latencies between seventeen and twenty-four seconds. It should be noted that these long latencies approach or perhaps exceed the limits for pauses in American English conversation. Because of the long delays, it was only by working back through the tapes that I was able to recognize these early utterances as imitation. As Brenda's speech develops from (012) to (051), there is a general trend toward shorter and shorter latencies.

The second thing to be noticed is that, whereas in the first session it was possible to find four fairly clear cases of imitation (there were others that some wider definitions might have included), in the last two sessions there was only one case each. It appears that direct phonetic imitation has declined in importance somewhat as BRENDA I has progressed.

V.2.3 Systematicity in Imitations

I suggested in Chapter 3 that the phonological study was largely based on spontaneous utterances. Now, we can return to look at the phonology of the few imitated utterances to see to what extent it varies from the system described previously. At first glance, it is clear that there is no very great difference. We do not find an abundance of velars or four-syllable utterances. In general, the same conditions hold here as in the productive system. Words are mostly monosyllables of CV shape. What can be noticed are several incipient changes in the phonological system.

As early as (021) there is [bau] for *book*. In (022) *boat* is imitated as [baæ]. In (032) and (041) there are two more examples of [b]. There are also several examples of [ʔ], [p], and [l] occurring as final consonants.

It should be remembered that in the phonology of tape (012) ⟨da⟩ was given as evidence for the nasal/oral split of the first consonant. Now it is seen that this ⟨da⟩ can be considered an imitation. However, by the next week (021) it has been incorporated into Brenda's spontaneous system. In the same way, it seems likely that the difficulty of the labial/dental opposition for the last session (051) can be cleared up somewhat with these examples. We can see that although, perhaps, Brenda does have an [m]/[n] distinction in (051), she is still working on the [b]/[d] distinction. It looks as if what is selected out for imitation by Brenda are just those distinctions she is in the process of developing. In the period between (021), when she has reached stage 2 of Jakobson's stages, and (S11), when she has reached stage 3, her system is in flux. During this time she becomes aware of the next contrast, perhaps first in receptive competence, and selects just those items that demonstrate this contrast for imitation. By this process she is able to learn the contrast finally for production.

V.2.4 Function of Imitation

I have suggested that an important function of imitation is to seek out examples of contrasts for practice and eventual incorporation into the child's own phonological system. Two of the features of these imitations indicate that this is the case. One is the long latency between the model and the imitation. This may indicate that the child has noticed a relevant model, but because it is not within her productive system it takes some time to process. It would not be surprising if this processing effectively blocked any other utterances on the part of the child or the hearing of any of the input speech in the interim. It is true that in the examples cited Brenda virtually blocked out any further input.

The second thing that would be expected is that the necessity of imitation would vary depending on what stage in development the child was in. We would suppose that when a child had recently acquired a contrast she would then be more interested in practicing that new acquisition than in seeking out new changes. This is one explanation that would be offered for the decrease in the number of imitations in BRENDA I. She is reaching a period in which stage 3 will be stabilized, and she is actively perfecting the system she has.

Example 15, Table 11, shows how the process of refinement takes place. It is repeated here.

```
(051)121   abə
     122   ada
                  (S)   She wants another one.
     123   ada
                  Atha?
     124   adδa
                  Ada.
```

There is still a slight processing delay. When Suzanne says "another," Brenda does not immediately correct, but there is a slight affrication in the stop in 123. Suzanne on her part corrects in the direction of Brenda's speech but stops short of going all the way to Brenda's [ada]. Then Brenda gets Suzanne's form and Suzanne gets Brenda's original form. It should be pointed out that in Hawaiian English *ada* is a stereotyped variable of Standard English *other*. This example shows that in the course of the eight weeks Brenda has gone from slow and perhaps difficult imitations to rather quick and subtle imitations. But these imitations only slightly expand the limits of her current phonological system.

V.3   Repetition vs. New Utterance—The Problem of Variation

In discussing the methodology of doing phonology on Brenda's speech, the problem was raised as to how to decide which utterances were repetitions of the "same" word and which utterances were new words. I felt that when utterances were said in a more or less close sequence, with approximately the same phonetic shape and an unvarying context, they could be taken as repetitions. In this section, some of the details and problems of that method are discussed.

First a note should be made about a certain type of circularity that will arise shortly in the discussion of constructions. If a sequence such as [nene . nene . nene] is taken as repetition of the same word, what is the basis for thinking later that [awau] in [nene . nene . awau] is not a repetition, but rather the introduction of a different word? The same context and conditions cannot be used for decisions in favor of repetition and decisions against it. Here, as in the problem of the intelligibility of words used spontaneously versus those used in imitation, we find that the linguist must make a judgment at some point in order to break the closed circle of the child's system. The means of judgment can be made somewhat explicit by saying that what is at least marginally acceptable to the adult system can be decided by reference to it. If we make that assumption, then we can say that we take as repetitions those utterances that maintain an intelligible limit of variation and do not overlap with other words in the supposed system.

V.3.1   Latency of Repetitions

This section will give some specification to the idea of a word being repeated in sequence. Table 12 is a list of some repeated words taken from tapes (012) and (051). It can be seen that for (012) there are two basic types of latencies—long and short. The long latencies are between $3\frac{1}{5}$ seconds and $8\frac{1}{5}$ seconds; the short are all $1\frac{3}{5}$ seconds. There are only three of the short type. The rest are long.

In (051) the same two categories hold except there are many in the short category (with $2\frac{4}{5}$ seconds as a maximum) and only a small number of long pauses. As can be seen from these examples, the timing of the short pauses has not varied importantly over the

TABLE 12. Repetitions in BRENDA II

Tape/Utterance	Word		Time between Repetitions
(012) 3, 4	nene	(2x)	$8\frac{1}{5}$
21, 22	da	(2x)	$1\frac{3}{5}$
59, 60, 60a, 61	nene	(4x)	$21\frac{4}{5}, 1\frac{3}{5}, 7\frac{2}{5}$
62, 63, 64	nene	(3x)	$3\frac{1}{5}, 1\frac{3}{5}$
(051) 6, 7	nene	(2x)	$2\frac{1}{5}$
15, 16	dædi	(2x)	$1\frac{2}{5}$
20, 21, 22	nene	(3x)	$2\frac{4}{5}, 1\frac{2}{5}$
27, 28, 29	awəu	(3x)	$1\frac{3}{5}, 2\frac{3}{5}$
30, 31, 32	dæyu	(3x)	$1, 8$
33, 34	awəu	(2x)	$2\frac{2}{5}$
36, 37	awəu	(2x)	$2\frac{2}{5}$
38, 39, 40, 41, 42, 43	awəu	(6x)	$2\frac{1}{5}, 2\frac{2}{5}, 4\frac{3}{5}, 2\frac{3}{5}, 3\frac{3}{5}$
46, 47, 48, 49, 50, 51, 52	dædi	(7x)	$11\frac{3}{5}, 4\frac{3}{5}, 2\frac{2}{5}, 1\frac{4}{5}, 8, 10\frac{1}{5}$
66, 67	lala	(2x)	2
93, 94, 95, 96, 97, 98	nau	(6x)	$2, 1\frac{2}{5}, 1, 1\frac{2}{5}, 1\frac{4}{5}$
134, 135, 136, 137, 138, 139, 140, 141	awəu	(8x)	$5\frac{4}{5}, 2\frac{1}{5}, 1\frac{4}{5}, 1\frac{4}{5}, 1\frac{4}{5}, 1\frac{4}{5}, 2\frac{1}{5}$

eight-week period. One second seems to be the lower limit on the short pauses (only two instances). On long strings such as (051)46 through 52, (051)93 through 98, and (051)134 through 141, there is a peculiar symmetry with the intervals shortening and then lengthening again.

V.3.2 The Place of Repetition in the System

The number of repetitions is an indication of a kind of development. It should be noticed that the four examples of (012) are exhaustive. Those of (051) are selected out of many more. Not included in Table 12 are data from (052) and (061) in which even greater extremes are reached. In those cases most of the words Brenda says are repeated. The maximum seems to be six to eight repetitions, but sequences of two or three repetitions are by far the most common. Of course there has been quite an increase in the total number of utterances in each session since the beginning, with sixty-six in (012), 183 in (061), and 399 in (052). What is clearly happening is that Brenda does not increase significantly the number of types but greatly increases the tokens. (See V.6.4 for a fuller discussion of types, tokens, and uses.)

V.3.3 Function of Repetition

There are a number of causes of a high number of tokens, that is, repetitions of the same word. One is that when Brenda says something there is no response, and so she says it again. Associated with this is the fact that it is difficult for others to understand her. A look at the transcriptions shows many instances of Brenda's utterance being followed by a request for repetition or clarification, such as "what?" or "doll?" or "you want?".

A further cause could be a difference in the latency of production interacting with conversational latencies. Adult speakers have quite definite intervals beyond which it is felt that a new utterance is called for. It could be that Brenda had said a word and the quick adult response might have been too soon for her to process. Meanwhile, she has begun the production of the repetition. This, of course, could be studied by looking at latencies in adult responses and then actively trying to alter the adult system in conversation with children. In VI.4.3 I will discuss another use of repetition, the introduction of a topic. This use, however, is relatively unimportant until near the end of BRENDA II and does not become widespread until BRENDA III.

Probably the most plausible explanation of this high number of repetitions is that Brenda is using them to learn phonology. If it is true, as I have suggested, that repetitions are a useful means of deciding about phonetic variability, there is no reason to suppose that this is not the case for Brenda as well. By keeping everything else constant (context, intent, etc.), she could vary the phonetic shape to see what gets understood. It may be too much to think that this is intentional, however. Probably it is a combination of the adult's lack of understanding, further prompting, and Brenda's experimentation that leads to this development of repetition.

V.4   Conclusion to Discourse Redundancies in BRENDA I

It has been shown that imitation and repetition are two phases of the same learning process. Imitation provides the means for the child to practice contrasts that are not yet within her own productive phonological system. Repetition provides the means for elaborating that system from within and testing it against the model system. It is interesting to notice the relative shift in importance of these two mechanisms between (012) and (051). In (012), imitation was considerably more frequent than in (051). For repetition just the reverse was the case. In light of this it would not be surprising to see the periodic waxing and waning of these two elements of adaptation as the developing system advances from stage to stage.

V.5   Imitation and Modeling in BRENDA II, Age 1;7.2 to 1;8.21

In BRENDA II, it has become more difficult to find clear cases of imitation. There may be several reasons for this. As I will show in V.5.4 below, the latency between the imitation and the word imitated has become quite short. This, coupled with the greatly increased vocabulary and fluency in its use, makes it hard to separate true imitations from simply appropriate responses to others' speech. On the other hand, although the latency may be quite small, apparently Brenda's memory has developed sufficiently to allow her to delay the imitation.

I want to recall the distinction I have made between an utterance that is an imitation and one that has been modeled. In either case, there has been an instance in another speaker's speech of the word the child says. To call an utterance "modeled" does not necessarily mean that it is an imitation. It only means that we cannot guarantee that it is not an imitation since a model was present. In the discussion that follows, utterances will be divided into those that are quite clearly imitations and those that only may have been imitated, that is, modeled utterances. Table 13 gives some examples of both kinds of utterances found in BRENDA II.

V.5.1   Obvious Imitations

There are several indications that a word is really imitated. One of these is when the suspected imitation immediately follows a model in the environment, but that model is of no direct relevance

TABLE 13. Imitation in BRENDA II

Example	Tape	Utterance	Time Lapse (Sec.)	Input Speech
E1	(071)			Mommy, you wanna play—pussy cat again?
			$1\frac{2}{5}$	
	190	pʰuʔsiʔ		
E2	(071)			You're gonna tape, right?
			$1\frac{2}{5}$	
	43	tʰeitʰ		
E3	(081)			Suzie!
			$1\frac{3}{5}$	
	125	čušiʔ		
E4	(091)			That's jack-o-lantern. Jack-o-lantern.
			$6\frac{2}{5}$	
			$\frac{4}{5}$	What's that?
	21	lɛ̃tʰɔ		
E5	(101) 44	eikʰ		
	45	eikʰ		
	46	eikʰ		
				Tamago?
			$4\frac{4}{5}$	
	47	mɔgu		
	48	magu		
	49	eikʰ		
E6	(101)			I can draw a better egg. Drew on your letters. Monster!
	50	m		
	51	eikʰ		
	52	eikʰ		
	53	eikʰ		
	54	eikʰ		

TABLE 13—*Continued*

Example	Tape	Utterance	Time Lapse (Sec.)	Input Speech
		55	eik^h		
		56	eik^h		
		57	mawnt^{h}u (3x)	$10\frac{3}{5}$	
E7	(121)70	baš		(laughing) You saw lady
	71	baš		wearing blanket on the bus.
				[bə ʔəs ʔɔ̃ ʔɔ̃ ʔ]
			$1\frac{2}{5}$	
	72	ba ʔəš		
E8	(131)			Next time I want some
				shoyu on it.
			$2\frac{1}{5}$	
	30	šiyo		
E9	(131)			Boy, you put so much
				shoyu.
			$2\frac{2}{5}$	
	71	mač		
E10	(131)			One.
			$\frac{3}{5}$	
	276	wən		Two.
			$1\frac{1}{5}$	
	277	t^{y}u		Three. (3 sec.) Three.
			$4\frac{3}{5}$	
	278	čič		Four.
			$2\frac{3}{5}$	
	279	fwa		Five.
			$\frac{4}{5}$	
	280	fai		

TABLE 13—*Continued*

Example	Tape	Utterance	Time Lapse (Sec.)	Input Speech
				Six.
			1	
	281	šɛʔkʰi		
				Seven.
			1	
	282	šedɛn		
			$1\frac{1}{5}$	
	283	sewɛn		
E11	(141)2	haidi:		
				Hide? What's hiding?
	3	brũ		
				Oh, the balloon? Where? Where is it? Where is it?
			$20\frac{4}{5}$	
	4	haidĩŋ		
E12	(141)			Where? Can't you find it?
			$2\frac{1}{5}$	
	15	faind		
	16	fain		
E13	(141)			It's almost nighttime? It's almost nighttime?
			$3\frac{2}{5}$	
	120	naitaim		
E14	(141)			Poor Brenda bumped her head. It hurt? Bump it again.
			$5\frac{3}{5}$	
	125	bəmp		
	126	hɛ		

TABLE 13—*Continued*

Example	Tape	Utterance	Time Lapse (Sec.)	Input Speech
E15	(141)			No, you can't step on my microphone!
			$2\frac{1}{5}$	
	173	məikrə̃ʔɔ̃		
				Microphone! Come on, say it right.
			$3\frac{4}{5}$	
	174	məikʸu		
	175	məikʰo		

to what Brenda is doing at the time. Example E13, Table 13 shows a case of this type.

The most frequent single type of clear imitation is that which is elicited by adults. About half of the total of imitations are of this type. It sometimes happens that Brenda uses a different word than expected and the adult corrects her. She then imitates this correction. E3 occurred when Brenda mistakenly called Suzanne Wendy. The group in E10 clearly shows how willing Brenda is to participate in this kind of imitative dialogue with Charlotte. In E4 we can see how this process works out on some occasions. The mother tells Brenda a word, repeating it several times. She then asks Brenda to name the object. Only a few examples have been given here. There were about 50 clear cases (out of a total of 2,940 utterances in BRENDA II).

A third type of imitation, which is considerably rarer, is that of a spontaneous imitation of some stressed word, as seen in E2, or the repetition of some word that is marked in some other way. E1 shows a case of the second type where Charlotte makes a pause before the imitated word.

Finally, there is one interesting example of a rather strange imitation, E7. Brenda says *bus* several times. The mother recalls the story of Brenda saying that the lady on the bus was wearing a blanket. The mother laughs when she says "bus," and Brenda immediately imitates the interrupted vowels in the mother's dangling pronunciation of *bus*. Since this is the only case of this kind, not too much should be made of it. It does, however, point up a rather subtle awareness of phonetic detail in imitation.

V.5.2 Modeling

There are some cases where a word occurs soon enough before Brenda says it, so that there is the possibility of imitation. E6 is a case of this sort. Brenda knows the word *monster* and has used it before on earlier tapes. When she says *monster* it is open to question whether this is a response in imitation of Charlotte's word or simply a response to the picture that Charlotte is drawing.

A second consideration has come up during the earlier discussion of phonology. Although in some cases it is quite difficult to claim that Brenda has directly imitated because of a time lapse or intervening speech, there is nevertheless a change in the phonological shape of her utterance, and this change is in the direction of the model. E11 is the example that was quoted above (III.8.1). Between my model *hiding* and Brenda's improved version of *hiding*, Brenda has said the word *balloon*. If this is imitation, it is delayed imitation.

It is not at all uncommon to find that Brenda's pronunciation improves even though there is a delay of several minutes, and the conversation has been about different things in the interval. This is a fairly strong indication that Brenda's mental representations of adult forms are quite mobile and susceptible to alteration, even though she does not immediately practice the form.

V.5.3 Position and Stress

I suggested in V.2.1 that the position and stress of the word imitated were important. Now we can see that for BRENDA II this idea must be modified. In the elicited and spontaneous imitations, the words imitated are either stressed or placed in a position of significance by pauses, as mentioned in E1. However, in the case of modeling it is not necessarily the modeled word that is stressed. In E9 it is *shoyu* that receives stress rather than *much*, which is the imitated word. Apparently by this stage Brenda can select utterances for imitation from the speech stream whether or not they are stressed.

V.5.4 Latency

In BRENDA I, I noticed that with development the latencies for imitations decreased. For these imitations in BRENDA II we can see that she has become quite adept. Some of them occur as quickly as within $\frac{3}{5}$ of a second, with rare cases showing a lapse of four to six seconds. It is interesting to note that in response to the mother's speech the latencies are shortest ($\frac{3}{5}$ to $1\frac{4}{5}$ seconds, typically). It appears that Brenda is "tuned" to her mother's speech. With other adults the latencies are slightly longer (1 to $2\frac{2}{5}$ seconds). This range of $\frac{3}{5}$ to $2\frac{2}{5}$ seconds covers over two-thirds of the total imitations for BRENDA II.

Now that we have seen that the latencies are normally quite short, we can see a reason for some of the longer ones that occur. In E10 when Brenda imitates *three* she has a $4\frac{3}{5}$ second delay. It is plausible that this is because *three* is a more difficult word for her than the words in the first two numbers. It should also be pointed out that she often says *one* and *two* spontaneously.

A second type of difficulty shows up in E5. Brenda has said *egg*. Suzanne says *tamago* (Japanese for 'egg'), and Brenda delays $4\frac{4}{5}$ seconds before imitating. It is likely that Brenda is familiar with this word, although she rarely volunteers any Japanese words. It could, perhaps, be a case of trying to reconcile these two words for the same object that causes the delay in this case.

One final case is that of E14. Apparently Brenda is imitating the longer phrase *bumped her head*, and to do this she has to produce two words, *bump* and *head*, in sequence, neither of which would be particularly hard for her. However, there is a $5\frac{3}{5}$ second delay in producing the sequence. This is the type of evidence for increased complexity that I point to later in VII.1 when I discuss words which serve as elements in constructions.

V.5.5 Systematicity of Imitation

As we have seen both in BRENDA I and in the discussion of phonology, the imitations Brenda makes do not differ widely from her phonological system at the time. They seem to add just those elements that are currently developing. E11 in which Brenda adds the velar nasal, or E12 where the final voiced stop occurs in the first instance and then disappears, gives evidence for this suggestion.

V.5.6 Function of Imitation

In V.5 I said that clear cases of imitation are somewhat harder to find in BRENDA II than in BRENDA I. Out of a total of 2,940 utterances, there were about fifty clear cases. We should not expect to answer many of the questions of Brenda's development by looking solely to these imitations. However, it can be seen that the imitations do have several uses in Brenda's system.

One of these uses is the practice of forms while the adult model is immediately present. This allows for the expansion of the phonological system. Related to this function is the simple increase of vocabulary. It is not to be supposed that every word must be imitated before becoming a part of Brenda's vocabulary, but apparently some of them are.

Another function of imitation may be useful in later syntactic constructions. In E8 and E9 the word imitated is semantically salient although in E9 it is not stressed. It may not necessarily be that Brenda has to imitate these words to learn about their salience, but their imitation in the context of a dialogue allows for further feedback and verification of her choice.

A final case that is important to mention is that of E15, which has already been discussed above (III.10). (141)173 was a spontaneous imitation of my *microphone*. Utterances 174 and 175 were emphatically elicited. It is interesting that form 174 took her longer than 173, although it was, in fact, shorter and more consistent with Brenda's system at that time. I mentioned above that after a two-month hiatus when I saw Brenda for the first time since (141) that as I took out my tape recorder she said [məik^{y}əfon]. The family can remember no cases in which Brenda would have heard the word in the interval. There is no tape recorder or microphone in the home. It is quite evident that Brenda had remembered the adult surface form until her own production limitations were reduced.

These imitations in BRENDA II do not represent a very large portion of the data. They do indicate, however, an important sensitivity to the speech environment, which is one of the undoubted requisites for language development.

V.6 Types of Repetition

I will turn now to the other aspect of discourse redundancy, repetition. In BRENDA I there was no need to distinguish types of repetition. However, in BRENDA II there seem to be two sometimes distinct types, phonological repetition and discursive repetition.

V.6.1   Phonological Repetition

The example I gave in III.6.1, in which Brenda successively approximates the adult surface form of the word *shoe*, is a clear instance of phonological repetition from (071). What follows is another example, this time from (141).

(141)108   giεuf
    109   giεv
    110   giv
    111   giv

Repetitions of this type are most common among spontaneous words. Notice that Brenda requires no prompting to continue altering the form. Also notice in both the case of *give* from (141) and *shoe* from (071) that once the correct form is reached it is repeated. This may be an indication that Brenda knows what it is she wants to say and when she has succeeded.

V.6.2   Discursive Repetition

Discursive repetition involves repetition until the word is understood and gets a response. The following example is from (111):

(111)1   fẽĩ   (Brenda is looking at electric fan)
    2   fæ̃
             (M)   Hm?
    3   fæ̃
             Bathroom?
    4   fanĩ
    5   faĩ
             Fan! Yeah.
    6   kʰu
             Cool, yeah. Fan makes you cool.

It is clear that Brenda persists in spite of the mother's misunderstanding until after 5 [faĭ] when the mother gets it right. Further evidence that she really is saying *fan* is that as soon as the mother guesses right Brenda is prepared with the comment, that is, that it is cool. This comment the mother understands immediately, and there is no need for repetition.

A second example from (111) shows even more definitely what Brenda is doing.

(111)	111	kʰa	(A car passes in the street.
	112	kʰa	R does not hear it at the time.)
	113	kʰa	
	114	kʰa	
			(R) What?
	115	gɔo	
	116	go	
			(S) x x x
	117	bəiš	
	118	bəiš	
	119	bəiš	
	120	bəiš	
	121	bəiš	
	122	bəiš	
	123	bəiš	
	124	bəiš	
	125	bəiš	
			(R) What? Oh, bicycle?
			Is that what you said?
	126	naʔ	
			No?
	127	naʔ	
			No—I got it wrong. (laugh)

When Brenda first says *car*, I don't understand, since I had not heard it. It was very clear on the tape, however. Brenda says it four times, and then as soon as I respond she changes to *go*. She says that twice until Suzanne says something which, unfortunately, is inaudible on the tape. Brenda then guesses correctly that we haven't understood and then says *bus*. This was verified from tape (121) in which she uses *bus* in the clear context of a story. When I suggest that she is

saying *bicycle*, she doesn't hesitate to say *not* and shakes her head
'no'. (Hawaiian English often has "not" as a one-word negative
indicating a denial of some assertion.)

What can be seen in this example is the fact that Brenda does
have definite intentions. She says the word until she gets the response,
and this response can be of two types. One type of response is to
simply say the word, thereby confirming that what she has said
translates to you in a certain way. A second type of response is just
to ask her if that's what she said. She apparently is ready to say when
it is wrong.

Of the repetitions in BRENDA II, this type is by far the most
frequent. However, it can be seen that the distinction between
discursive repetition and phonological repetition is not always easy
to maintain. As an example of the mixture of the two types we can
look at the following from (071):

> (Brenda has been drawing pictures. She
> draws one she says is a ⟨wowow⟩, i.e.,
> a dog.)

(071)	366	bəm
	367	bəm
	368	bam
	369	bəu

(M) Hm?

	370	boĭ
	371	boni
	372	bəunĭ
	373	boni

Brown? Hm?

	374	ræuš
	375	rous
	376	rəuh

Ralph? Yes, Ralph is a dog.

In this case Brenda's *bone* improves somewhat but the mother
never succeeds in understanding *bone*. Then Brenda does an
interesting thing. She gives up on bone and starts saying *Ralph*,
the name of a dog that belongs to Brenda's cousins. This is further
evidence that Brenda was in fact saying *bone*.

V.6.3   Latency

It is clear by now that Brenda has developed a considerable fluency since BRENDA I. It can be seen in the latencies between repetitions. In the first case of the phonological repetitions, these lapses are very short. In the *shoe* example quoted we find the following intervals between the first seven utterances: $\frac{3}{5}$, $\frac{4}{5}$, $\frac{3}{5}$, $\frac{3}{5}$, $\frac{3}{5}$, $\frac{4}{5}$ seconds. There is a lapse of $1\frac{1}{5}$ seconds while Suzanne says *shoes*. Then between the last three words we find $1\frac{1}{5}$ and 1 seconds. These lapses are quite typical of phonological repetitions. There is only a short breath taken between.

In one interesting case, (071)59, the pause gets put in the wrong place with the result that the final consonant of one word gets placed at the beginning of the next word.

(071)59   hæˀ:thæˀ   (i.e., *hat.hat.*)

In this case the pause of $\frac{4}{5}$ seconds is that which is typical between words.

In discursive repetitions the latencies are only slightly longer than for phonological repetitions. Typically they are around one second, ranging between $\frac{4}{5}$ and $1\frac{4}{5}$ seconds. They are rarely longer than that.

V.6.4   Place of Repetition in the System

Having described the different forms of repetitions, we should now see to what extent it is representative of speech in BRENDA II. First, a three-way distinction must be made among "type," "token," and "use." An example will illustrate these terms.

(141)2   hiding
      3   balloon
      4   hiding
      5   hiding
      6   hiding
      7   hiding
      8   hiding
      9   hiding

In this example there are two "types"—*hiding* and *balloon*. There are eight "tokens"—one token of the type *balloon* and seven tokens of the type *hiding*. There are three "uses"—one use of *balloon* and two uses of *hiding*. In the first use of *hiding* there is one token, but in the second use of *hiding* there are six tokens or, also in the terms of this study, repetitions. It is important to notice that if repetitions are derived by simply dividing tokens by types, the number of repetitions for a particular use is obscured.

Of the 63 uses of words in (071), 17 were not repeated; that is, they occurred singly. Fourteen received one repetition, and 12 received two repetitions. The maximum repetition was 14, but there were cases with 9, 10, and 11 repetitions.

To summarize these data for (071), we can say that about one-fourth of the words of (071) occurred singly. About forty percent received one or two repetitions. That is to say, when most of the words in (071) were used they were repeated, and the most common pattern was one or two repetitions.

By (141) the situation had changed somewhat. There are 325 tokens and 71 types. Of the 71 types, there were 129 uses. Sixty-one of these occurred singly. Thirty had one repetition and 22 had two repetitions. That is to say, just a little less than half occurred singly, and of the remaining half most occurred with only one or two repetitions. The maximum was eight repetitions.

Table 14 summarizes these data in graph form. As these graphs indicate, there has been a considerable reduction in repetition during BRENDA II.

V.6.5   Function of Repetition

Since one function of repetition is to successively improve the phonetic form of Brenda's words, it is clear that repetition should decrease as Brenda's phonological system approaches the adult system. As she continues to develop her pronunciation skills, she can get to the intelligible form quicker. A second function of repetition has been seen to be that of getting a response from the listener. As Brenda's phonological system improves and as her vocabulary increases, her speech is more readily intelligible. The result of this is a reduction in the number of repetitions needed to get others to understand. It can be seen, then, that the reduction in the amount of repetition demonstrates that one function of repetition—intelligibility—is being met in other ways by the end of BRENDA II.

TABLE 14. Frequency of Repetitions

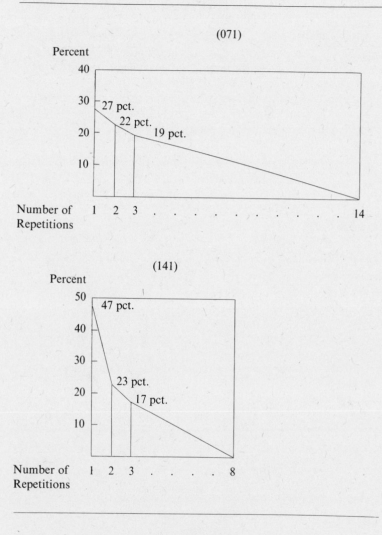

(071)

(141)

V.7 Conclusion to Discourse Redundancies

In the discussion of imitation, we saw that imitation in
BRENDA II was getting rarer. We also saw one example of the

imitation of a longer sequence, that is, (141)125 and 126 [bəmp.hɛ]. Further, we can see that repetition is getting rarer. This is an indication on the one hand that at the level of single words Brenda is achieving considerable intelligibility. In the discussion of construction, I will show that this is an indication of a shift of focus to a somewhat broader level, the level of the several word construction—that is, vertical construction.

CHAPTER VI

Discourse

VI.1   Dialogue in BRENDA I, Ages 1;0.2 to 1;1.22

I am using the term "discourse" to refer to two somewhat
different things. The first meaning is that of a series of utterances
by the same speaker that form some kind of connected whole.
Monologue might be an appropriate term for an adult, but it seems
quite exaggerated to call anything a child as young as Brenda could
produce a monologue. The other type would be called dialogue.
For Brenda dialogue seems more appropriate, although in the
earliest part of this study, BRENDA I age 1;0.2 to 1;1.22, there is
very little that one would want to call dialogue. There is an occa-
sional utterance that with some stretch of the imagination might
fall into this category. Utterance (1) below is the only example
offered here. On the whole, at the beginning of our study it is
difficult to see anything but imitations or words in response to
objects or events. Further on, however, Brenda does start to develop
the ability to respond to speech with speech. The examples given
here are divided into two groups. The first three are rather marginal;
the other two, (4) and (5), are good examples of the type of dialogue
between Brenda and adults that has developed by the end of
BRENDA I. The first example (1) is from (012). Utterances (2) and
(3) are from (061), while (4) is from two weeks before, (051). Finally,
(5) is from (Sll), the very last tape of this series.

(1) (012)   (R) Do you want some more?
        46   neneneu   (i.e., juice)

_____

(2) (061)6   hævo   (B playing with telephone—
        7   ye: holding receiver to ear)
        8   edi
                                   (C) Daddy, yeah.

_____

(3) (061)   (B playing with telephone)
                                   (R) You disconnected the phone.
        30   əidaʔa   (B pushing away receiver)
                                   (C) You through, yeah? Yeah?
                                        You through, yeah?

_____

(4) (051)   (B, M, R looking at picture
                                        magazine)
        53   ala
                                   (M) What's that? Hm. Sausage.
                                        Un. Yum-yum.
                                   (R) What's this, Brenda?
        54   ælə
                                   (M) Um.
        55   æyɨ
                                   (M) You want? That's French
                                        fries.
                                   (R) Um. What's this?
                                   (M) Mm.
        56   m
                                   (M) (laugh)
                                   (R) (laugh) I agree. It looks
                                        good.
        57   mæ
                                   (M) manman. (i.e., 'solid food')
                                        Um hm.
        58   məmæ
                                   (M) Yeah.
        59   mɛmæ
        60   ava

		(M) You want? Oh, can't eat from that.
		(R) Oh, look, Here's some fish.
61	dædi	
		(R) What?
62	awəu	
		(M) Hm? Oh, yes. That's for Daddy. Yes, for Daddy.

(5) (S11)   (M) Uh. Three. Three pennies. See? Have one more?

205 ivəu

Chodai. Chodai. (i.e., 'please give it to me.')

206 iwəu

Um hm.

207 dəwo

Thank you.

208 da?

One more.

209 iw?

Thank you.

210 duo

One more.

211 dowəu

Pen? You write. You write with pen. Yeah.

Utterance (1) might be a case of the answer to a question. There is the somewhat characteristic time lag—20⅘ seconds in this case. This first example is from the earlier tape. The other examples are at least two months later. Utterances (2) and (3) might better be called self-accompanying dialogue. In (2) Brenda is pretending a phone conversation. Notice the correct use of the ritual *hello*. She is pretending to be talking with her father. Utterance (3) sounds very much like *all done* which would certainly be correct in the situation. In both (2) and (3), notice Charlotte's interpretive role. She is playing with Brenda and not trying to explain to anyone else.

The conversations of (4) and (5) are the only two examples of dialogue of this length. Notice in (4) the prompting of the conversation by the adults. By way of contrast notice that in (5) this type of prompting is absent. Brenda's words are taken just as she says them, and the mother responds as if her understanding were complete. The mother reported, however, that she didn't really understand anything that Brenda had said. It is interesting to notice that in this case where the discourse is quite fluent the content is highly unintelligible, even more so than for other uses of speech on the same tape. One gets the impression that to accomplish both tasks—discourse structuring and phonological structuring—at the same time is not possible at this stage. This suggests that there is an interaction in complexity between phonological structure and discourse structure so that an increase in one causes a decrease in the other. This same phenomenon is discussed later (VII.1) with vertical construction.

I suggested in the discussion of phonology (see especially III.5 and III.10) that some concept of successive approximation was needed to explain the child's developing phonological system. In the discussion of imitation a type of system was suggested in which the child would imitate just those elements she was in the process of learning. Here it seems consistent to propose that on this level of the higher context of language a similar type of development takes place. It is plausible to suggest that Brenda has first developed a basic phonological system, one that works well enough to make her utterances intelligible to adults (at least concerned adults). Then on the basis of that quite simple system she begins to develop the socially interactive uses of speech without particular attention to the phonological form or semantic content of the words. Here again it seems that Brenda is developing her language by first focusing on one aspect and then another, and while focusing on one aspect she of necessity temporarily suspends or at least decreases activity in another.

VI.2   Stories in BRENDA II, Ages 1;7.2 to 1;8.21

By BRENDA II the situation has changed considerably. I found many examples of stories (monologues) and conversations (dialogues) as well as the harangue that follows. In spite of the restrictions of a rather limited vocabulary and expressive means, we can see how well Brenda is able to piece these few words into an urgent demand for attention. In this section I have changed to an orthographic translation of my transcription for ease in under-standing the flow. (It should be remembered that the translation here misrepresents the actual phonetics.)

(6)   (131)   (C and B are playing in the
                                 sandbox at making sand
                                 cupcakes. C began to scoop up
                                 sand from where B was playing.)
                             (C)   I'm making plenty cupcakes
                                 so I'm trying to get plenty.

        141   plenty
        142   plenty
        143   plenty
        144   plenty
        145   plenty
        146   fight
        147   fight
        148   no fair
        149   fight

I have said that in **BRENDA II** Brenda tells stories. Stories are taken to mean sequences in which the words Brenda uses are part of a larger whole that taken together has a unified meaning. In telling them she is not significantly assisted by another speaker. In the examples that follow these points will be easier to see.

(7)   (081) 163   tape   (Pointing to recording tape)
              164   tape
              165   tape
              166   tape   (Pointing to band-aid tape)
              167   tape
              168   Brenda
              169   hurt
              170   Mommy
              171   Mommy

172   band-aid [bænĩʔĩ]
173   hurt
174   hurt

The gist of the story is clear. The mother had put a band-aid on Brenda's sore. Incidentally, this was not something that I knew before Brenda mentioned it.

(8) (091)44   duck
                        (M) Hm?
     45   duck
     46   swim
     47   swim
     48   swim
     49   swim
     50   duck
                        Can duck swim?
     51   Brenda
                        Brenda swims?
     52   Mommy
     53   swim
     54   swim
                        Mommy swims too.
     55   Charlotte
                        Un hm. Charlotte swims too.

This is not as clearly a "story" as (7). However, it is Brenda who leads, and it is common for the mother and her two children to go to the beach.

(9) (111)15   nen night   (B reaching for cushion and
                                 pretending to sleep)
     16   daddy
     17   daddy
                        (M) Yeah, Daddy nennen (i.e.,
                            'sleep') on that last night.

In this example Brenda is telling us about the nap her father took and then demonstrates by pretending to sleep.

(10) (121)   (M) ... long skirt you know and
                                   the pattern it was a check

just like a blanket—
Charlotte's blanket and
she said, "Lady, blanket,
blanket." She thought lady
was wearing blanket.

49 Brenda
50 sleeping

Hm? Yeah, you thought
lady was wearing blanket,
didn't you?

51 bus
52 bus

Yeah, on the bus, hm?

What is interesting about this story is that Brenda is talking about sleeping on the bus which is more or less not understood by the mother. Later after making the transcription of the tape I asked the mother how they went to the doctor's office and if Brenda had slept in the office or on the bus. The mother reported what Brenda had told me: She always falls asleep when they ride on the bus.

(11) (121)   (B is holding a porcelain bank in
                                the shape of a rabbit)
     166 rabbit
     167 rabbit
                          (R) Yeah.
     168 daddy
     169 daddy
                               Oh, that's his bank.
     170 playing
     171 playing
     172 playing
                               Is that your daddy's bank?
     173 bank
     174 Brenda

The story as reported by the mother is that the evening before the father had played with Brenda and Charlotte while the mother was out. They had been playing with the rabbit bank which was not the father's bank but Charlotte's.

VI.3   Conversations in BRENDA II, Ages 1;7.2 to 1;8.21

It is obvious that in the stories above there is never a complete independence from interaction with other speakers. In the conversations this interaction is at a much higher level. This is by far the most common type of discourse. Because so many examples of this type of interaction are given throughout this study only three will be given here.

(12) (081)			
		(M)	Tell Ron what swims, Brenda.
47	turtle		
			What can swim?
		(C)	Turtle she said.
		(M)	Um hm.
48	swim		
			Yeah.
49	swim		
			What else can swim?
50	fish		
51	fish		
52	water		

In (12) we see a type of conversational prompting that is often used between Brenda and her mother.

(13) (111)			
			(R, M, S are all sitting on the floor eating ice cream and temporarily ignoring tape recorder and notebook in which contextual notes were usually written)
176	tape		(B trying to move tape recorder)
177	tape		
178	word		(B holding mike up to S's mouth)
		(S)	Hm?
179	word		
180	word	(R)	She said, "word."
181	word	(M)	She wants you to say a word.
182	word		
		(R)	Yeah, she says—she holds it up to Suzie like that.

183	paper		
184	paper	(B giving notebook to S)	
185	paper		
186	paper		
187	paper	(R)	What's wrong? You think we're not doing our job just 'cause we're eating ice cream?
188	pen	(B gives pen to S)	
189	pen		
		(R to S) See? Now do your job! Pretty soon she's gonna give me an exam.	
190	tape		
191	tape		
		(R)	Yeah. O.K. Everything's under control. We're doing it all right.

This example is strong evidence of the awareness Brenda has of what we were doing and the functioning of the various elements of the recording session (for Bloom's contrasting point of view see II.1.3). It also shows how well she can participate with adults in a conversation of her own direction.

(14) (121)67	Kimby		
		(M)	What about Kimby?
68	close [koš]		
			Closed? What did she close, hm?

This final example is given to show the basic structure that can be seen in many of these conversations. Brenda begins by saying some word. This word is taken by the adult as the topic of a topic-comment pair. The adult shows in one way or another that the word has been understood and gives the signal for Brenda to elaborate. Brenda then goes on to the comment. This example demonstrates the way in which the discourse is patterned and segmented in many cases.

VI.4   The Initiation of Conversation

These stories and conversations indicate that by BRENDA II Brenda has gained a fair ability to interact with adults. This ability to interact implies the knowledge of at least some interaction rules. The fact that most interactions begin with Brenda's utterances as a topic implies that she has some ability to initiate interactions. To look at her initiation of conversations, I will first present data from the most developed data I have, BRENDA IV, since in BRENDA IV she showed a remarkably full control of these initiations. Then I will trace this development back through BRENDA III, BRENDA II and BRENDA I.

VI.4.1   Initiations in BRENDA IV, Age 2;0.12

Tape (171) begins as follows. Brenda came out of the bedroom and I turned on the tape recorder.

(15) (171)1   hi!

    (R)   Hi. How're you doing?
    (R to S) Let's see, piece of paper.
    Tri-X.

    2   hi!   (R to B) Hi. Hi. How are you.
    Been a long time since you
    saw this set up, isn't it?

Schegloff (1972) has pointed out that conversational openings normally follow a regular sequence. First one speaker gives a summons which requests the right to talk. A second speaker gives an answer that grants the right to talk to the first speaker. The first speaker, the summoner, then introduces the topic. This is followed by the conversation itself. When an answer does not occur the summons is usually repeated. It seems quite clear that Brenda considers *hi* in this case to be a summons because when I continue talking to Suzanne instead of to Brenda, Brenda repeats the summons. It also seems clear that I consider *hi* to be a greeting rather than a summons since a greeting requires only acknowledgment but no further interaction. Notice my *Hi. Hi.* which sounds to me now as though I am saying, "I said *Hi*, didn't you hear me?"

During the next hour, Brenda uses this *hi* seven times with me. In most cases I answer it as if it were a greeting but Brenda continues trying to talk to me. It is evident that for Brenda at this stage *hi* is a summons.

A second word which is very frequent is *here*. Brenda says *here* twenty-two times in one hour, each time handing or trying to hand something to the receiver. On one level, Brenda's use of *here* can be seen to be the performance of the speech act of handing (of course, with the accompanying behavioral component of handing). But it is hard to account for twenty-two instances of handing within an hour in this way alone. On another level, however, *here* can be seen to be a summons which is quite effective. In fact, it is much more effective than *hi*.

The conditions on handing will show why this should be so. Among many conditions two seem to be crucial; one is that the receiver must acknowledge that he has received the object (by taking it and usually by speech as well) and the other is that the hander is required to give further instructions. That is, in acknowledging receipt of the object the receiver grants the hander the right to interaction, specifically to say why the object was handed. In saying why the object was handed, the hander reserves the right to introduce a topic. This further confirms that *here* is used as a summons.

On the basis of these observations we can see that Brenda may use *hi* and *here* as summonses when she is initiating interactions. What happens when someone else tries to initiate interactions with Brenda? Two examples will illustrate what happens.

(16) (171)   (R)   What you doing over here,
                          Brenda? You still drink your
                          milk out of a bottle?
     181   here (handing the mike to R)
                          O.K. O.K.
     (171)   (R)   What's my name?
            (speaks to herself)
                          Brenda, my name's Ron.
            (continues speaking
            to herself)
     110   here (handing film can to R)
                          Thank you. My name's Ron,
                          remember that?

111   hi

Hi.   O.K.   O.K.

In both of these cases I try to summon Brenda. She does not answer (which would acknowledge my right to introduce the topic). Instead she returns with her own summons. This guarantees that although I have tried to initiate the interaction Brenda is officially marked as the initiator and therefore may introduce the topic. Her persistence in this is shown by her summons *hi* when I have persisted, quite egocentrically, in trying to introduce my name as the topic. Brenda refuses to grant me that privilege and my acceptance is indicated by saying *O.K. O.K.*

This use of *hi* and *here* is restricted, however, to interactions involving me, Suzanne, and for *here* only, Charlotte. Brenda's interactions with her mother generally begin with the introduction of a topic. It is as if the right to talk was permanently established between Brenda and her mother. (An informal comparison with the data collected by Ann Peters from a child with a Vietnamese mother indicates that this special status of the mother may be true of only Brenda's mother or, more generally, of the Japanese mother.) This special status of Brenda's mother enables her to act as a mediator between Suzanne or me and Brenda as the following two examples show.

(18) (171)		(S)	What's your sister's name?
	(silence)		
		(M)	What is your sister's name?
61	Charlotte		
(19) (171)		(R)	What's your Daddy's name, Brenda?
	(silence)		
		(M)	What is your Daddy's name?
104	(gives name)		
			(interaction between B and R continues)

In (18) Brenda responds to Suzanne's question only when the mother asks (and slightly rephrases) it. In (19), which is nearly identical, this mediation is sufficient to establish the state of talk between Brenda and me, and this interaction continues without the further mediation or presence of the mother. In these cases the mediation of the mother allows the topic introduced by Suzanne or me to stand, whereas in unmediated interactions Brenda must control the topic.

Now that we have seen how Brenda uses *hi* and *here* and with whom, we still need to see if Brenda has other means of requesting the right to talk. In one case while handing a book to me Brenda says, *I like read my teddy bear.* The normal sequence of summons/answer/topic is short-circuited here when Brenda introduces the topic at the time of the summons. Handing, then, may also occur without being accompanied by the word *here* as long as the topic is also introduced. That is, the speech act *here* and the action of handing are, in fact, separable in some cases, and either *here* plus handing or handing plus topic may function as a summons.

Once the right to talk is established there are still momentary lapses after which Brenda needs to reassert her participation. For example, Brenda appears to consider herself permanently in a state of talk with her mother, but sometimes her mother is actually talking to someone else. In such cases where the mother is not speaking to Brenda but Brenda is audience (or a possible participant) to the interaction Brenda uses repetition to regain the floor as in the following example.

(20) (171)

(C)	We should get the Snoopy toothbrush.
(M)	You saw that too, huh?
(C)	Yeah.
(M)	Somebody told me about it. On T.V.?
(C)	Yeah.
(R)	Snoopy toothbrush. What's it like?
(C)	You brush your teeth. You put on top, you put it on top of the toothbrush and brush with it.

175 Mommy have too, eh?

                              (M) Hm?
176 ﹜ Mommy have
        too

                              Mommy doesn't have—
                              Snoopy toothbrush.

177   Daddy have

                              No. Nobody has in our
                              house.

There is a special condition, however, that shows up when Brenda is excluded as a possible participant. Brenda's speech becomes quite unintelligible. An example of this was a stretch of wholly unintelligible speech while her mother was speaking Japanese on the phone. No one else was able to gain access to Brenda during this time and yet she continued to speak. Another example of this occurred when Brenda and I were interacting. I spoke several sentences in an aside to Suzanne and during this time Brenda said several things which are quite unintelligible. These lapses suggest that Brenda considers herself to be in interaction with a receiver but is also aware of the uselessness of speaking clearly to a receiver who is not really interacting. In every case, when the interruption ends, Brenda immediately returns to speaking clearly.

With one exception these observations can be summarized as follows:

(1) When the right to talk has not been established, Brenda uses *hi*, *here*, or the combination of handing plus topic to initiate interactions with Suzanne and me.
(2) With the mother the right to talk is permanently established.
(3) With Charlotte the right to talk may or may not be permanently established since *here* was only used a few times and when it was it failed.
(4) When the right to talk temporarily lapses but Brenda is still audience to the interaction, she regains the floor by repeating her utterance.
(5) When the right to talk temporarily lapses and Brenda is excluded as participant, she becomes unintelligible until the right to talk is reestablished.

The single exceptional situation is the "book game." This is the familiar "game" of an adult saying, *What's X* or *That's X* while going through a book with a child while the child imitates or responds in some way. There is one long section, about half of the total tape, in which Brenda and I are playing this game. At one point the following interchange takes place:

(21) (172)   (R)   What's this?

152   dat a—

                      (C)   This is rainbow trout?

                      (R)   Yeah. This is a rainbow trout.

             (C continues and B goes to another room)

Then a little later:

(22) (172)   (C)   Angry fish, ang.

                      (R)   Angel fish.

5   (C)   Angelfish. You like angel fish?

15   I like angel fish!

                      We got a play one.

                      We got a play kind.

                      We have a play kind.

                      Mommy, what happened to my fishes

156   dere   (C runs off)

         (B and R continue book game)

What is interesting in the book game is that participants do not need to establish the right to talk. Charlotte's entry into the game displaces Brenda and later Brenda's entry displaces Charlotte. There is apparently a two-participant rule that prohibits more than one child at a time. Not only that, the right to talk is established for the position or role of player in the game, not for the person in that role. It is like substitution of quarterbacks in football. Play is not backed up to start again but continues without consideration of the individuals.

What is exceptional about this book game is that during play the interactions between Brenda and me are like those between

Brenda and her mother elsewhere. This suggests that the restrictions on initiation of interactions apply to my role as visitor rather than to me as a person. It further suggests that one should say not that Brenda considers her mother to be permanently available for talk but that Brenda expects the person in the role of mother or caretaker to be permanently available for talk.

VI.4.2   Initiations in BRENDA III, Age 1;10.13, 1;10.17

The tapes of BRENDA III (15 and 16) were made a month and a half earlier. These data give further support to the idea that Brenda's interaction rules apply to roles rather than persons. First, however, it is necessary to sketch out Brenda's use of summonses for this period. In tape 16 there are no uses of *hi*. *Here* is used as in tape 17 accompanied by handing, and it is, in fact, used as a summons. In the discussion above, I suggested that *here* was more effective than *hi* as a summons because it included a behavioral summons. Tape 16 indicates that *here* may also be more primitive than *hi* in its use as a summons.

Handing by itself, that is without the uttering of *here*, does not constitute a summons. No conversation follows and Brenda makes no attempt to repeat the summons. In one case, Brenda introduces a topic (tape recorder) first by saying *tape corder* three times then simultaneously saying *Ron* and handing me the microphone. I say *O.K.* in acknowledgment and Brenda says *Ron talk*, that is, she gives the instruction about what to do with it. In this case, it is repetition plus calling by name plus handing that constitutes the summons. Apparently in BRENDA III, Brenda uses more to do less than in BRENDA IV.

The question can now be asked: Why should *here* be a more basic summons than *hi*? It may be because handing as a behavior has a set of conditions that guarantee behavioral interaction. I suggest that handing as a speech act (*here*, and in some earlier tapes, *give*, *some*) is symbolizing this behavior, whereas the other main summons *hi* does not symbolize any nonspeech behavior. I think this approach is in keeping with Piaget's position that symbolization develops out of sensorimotor behavior. I think it is reasonable to conceive of this physical action of handing and the consequent behavioral interaction as being more primitive than more purely speech-based interactions.

In tape 16, there are several attempts to set up the book game, two failures and one success. In the first I try to start the game as follows:

(23) (R) Help me read this book, Brenda. (repeated several times)
What's this?

(162) (silence)

About twenty minutes later the following interchanges take place:

(24) (R) (talking to M)
(162) Mommy
read dat
book
(M) What book is this?
[pi?]taro (R) (continues talking to M)
(M) Momotaro (a Japanese story about "Peach Boy")
come (3x)
flying
(M) What's flying?

In this sequence, Brenda succeeds in establishing some interaction with her mother, but I do not easily give up my previously established interaction that does not include Brenda as a participant. The mother is caught in between us and succeeds in giving an answer to Brenda, but it is a stalling answer.

About three or four minutes later the following sequence takes place:

(25) (162) (sneeze) (2x)
(R) Bless you, Brenda.
Ron read
O.K.
Ron
O.K.
(book game follows)

By the time the book game gets established, it has taken an attempt by me in which I indicate to Brenda my availability to play, an attempt by Brenda in which she tries to engage the mother in the game, and finally, a third attempt in which both Brenda and I show our mutual availability to begin the game. Once established, the game goes on for about fifteen minutes. In this context it can be seen that even Brenda's quite unintentional sneeze could function as a summons in setting up an interaction. This is probably true, however, only given the prior events that indicated readiness on both our parts to take the book game roles.

As in BRENDA IV, in this tape, the intelligibility of Brenda's speech is affected by the participant status of her interlocutor although not to the same extent. There is an episode in which Brenda and Charlotte are playing with a doll that has recorded messages that can be played by pulling a string. During this entire sequence, Brenda's speech is quite unintelligible. I suggest that this is very much like what happens when the mother is speaking on the telephone in (171) or when someone Brenda is speaking with turns to exclude her in an aside to another speaker. The doll appears to be speaking but does not respond to Brenda or interact in any way predictable to Brenda. By being sender but not receiver, the doll effectively excludes Brenda from interaction and the effect of this is Brenda's unintelligibility. A later case is when Brenda and Charlotte have been playing the Sesame Street game. I begin a conversation with Charlotte, and Brenda's speech becomes, again, quite unintelligible. Notice, however, that in (24), cited above, Brenda's speech remains intelligible even in the context of her mother's stalling answers.

Finally, in this tape there are a few cases of what I have called imaginative play. In these cases, Brenda is fantasizing on pretended events and talks without any evidence of seeking participant status with anyone present. Her speech cannot be related to any topic currently available or to any observable context, and she does not seem to be affected by lack of response from other speakers.

Tape 15 was recorded under different conditions from the other tapes of this study. The situation was a family party. There were around thirty people present, including aunts, uncles, and cousins. At the time of the recording Brenda was taking a bath. About five or six girl cousins were with her by the bathtub playing and talking. Suzanne was the senior cousin present throughout. The mother and I as well as Brenda's father came into the room and stayed for brief periods.

This change of situation dramatically indicates that Brenda's rules of interaction apply to roles rather than persons. Interactions between Brenda and her mother are much like those in the other recordings. Brenda simply begins to speak to her mother without previous summons/answer sequences. What is striking is that in this situation Brenda grants Suzanne the same privilege. There are several types of evidence for this. One is that throughout the bathtub scene Brenda simply talks to Suzanne without prior summons/ answer sequences. A second type of evidence is that speech with others, such as with her father and me, can only be mediated through Suzanne. In the case of Suzanne, this is quite different from the interactions four days later on tape 16 where Suzanne is treated as a visitor, requiring summons/answer sequences or mediation by the mother. In the case of the father, who normally interacts in the caretaker role, it constitutes a considerable restriction. There is apparently no appropriate role for either the father or me in bathroom interactions with Brenda, and Brenda's resistance to granting interaction rights indicates her awareness of this. Suzanne's role as person in charge of the bathing is a familiar one to Brenda. Suzanne is acceptable to Brenda in the caretaker role, particularly in the absence of the mother who is quite occupied in her role of hostess.

VI.4.3 Initiations in BRENDA II, Age 1;7.2 to 1;8.21

Tape (141) at the end of BRENDA II begins with the mother trying to prompt Brenda to say *hi* to Suzanne and me. This prompting fails. The situation indicates, however, that it fails not out of Brenda's ignorance of *hi* but out of her awareness of what saying *hi* entails. We had arrived in the house while Brenda was sleeping. When she woke and came to the living room, I turned on the tape recorder. At the time of the mother's prompting, Brenda had not yet spoken to anyone. She is clearly avoiding interaction. Her avoidance indicates that at (141) Brenda's knowledge of *hi* is functional to some extent.

One use of *hi* almost an hour later further confirms this. It also indicates that it is not only speech interaction that is involved. The following interchange took place between Suzanne and Brenda.

(26)   (142)   hi

(S)   Hi.
coming (running out of room)
Coming. (following after B)

In this case, *hi* is used to initiate a game of chase.

There were no uses of the word *here* in this recording but handing did occur as a summons. Brenda said *Suzie* eight times and *give* four times as she walked across the room and handed Suzanne a book to read. The observation that in BRENDA III Brenda used more to do less is further borne out here by the number of repetitions necessary to do the same thing as *here* plus handing accomplished three months later in BRENDA IV.

The behavior based interaction following *hi* above is typical of several other interactions. In these cases, it was a behavior (e.g., bumping her head against a wall when she fell, or threatening to step on the tape recorder) that functioned as a summons in initiating the interaction. In general, one gets the feeling in comparing (14) and (17) that in (17) speech interactions have subsidiary behaviors while in (14) it is the behaviors that have a subsidiary speech component.

Part of the evidence for this is the difficulty adults have in engaging Brenda in largely speech-based interactions. There is a much higher percentage of "soliloquies" in which there is no connection between Brenda's speech and the speech of others. Rather, we find the speech to be related to ongoing activities or behavior. The clearest example of the type of noninteractive speech that occurs shows up in the following interchange.

(27)   (141)   (C)   It's almost nighttime?
                              It's almost nighttime?
                        (M)   Yes! It's almost nighttime.
          120   nighttime

It was Halloween, and Charlotte was supposed to be napping to prepare for the evening's activities. She and her mother were two rooms away from where Brenda was being recorded, yet Brenda echoes the salient word in the interchange between Charlotte and her mother. She does not comment any further. She does not leave where she was to increase her involvement in the Charlotte/ mother interaction. In short, she is not interacting but simply speaking.

A brief book game takes place in (141) that further indicates the roles of the players. In the book game of (17), there was a substitution of children in the child role. In this case, I switch with Suzanne with no change in the flow of the game.

In studying the data of BRENDA III and BRENDA IV, I had wondered about *hey* as a possible summons. In (142) there is an interchange that perhaps indicates why it does not occur later as well as indicating that the assumption that Brenda and her mother are in a permanent state of interaction was not always so.

(28) (142)   x x x (3x)

	(M)	Look at all the candy.
hey!	(S)	(laughs)
x x x	(M)	Hm? Hey!?
mama		
		Yosh. You don't call
		Mommy Hey!

It is not entirely clear whether the mother objects to the use of the word *hey* or to the use of summons in beginning interactions with her. Whatever the case, *hey* does not occur again in my data—nor does a summons occur in Brenda's interactions with her mother.

In tape (071) at the beginning of BRENDA II, the study of the initiation of interactions is difficult for two reasons. One reason is that Brenda's utterances are so short and difficult to understand that most of the interchanges actually seem to be new events. That is, it is difficult to see that any sequence of interchange constitutes an interaction of some longer, more connected kind. The second problem (which may only be another aspect of the first) is that there is much "soliloquizing." That is, it is difficult to argue for any connection between the speech of Brenda and anyone else.

The example that follows can be used to illustrate.

(29) (071)   (R) What's that?
    36   ṇ ṇ gɔdə?   Yeah, that's tape recorder.

My use of *that* implies that I am not introducing the topic but that Brenda's attention is already focused on the tape recorder. It seems plausible that Brenda would have said the same thing anyway, without my question. What I do, in fact, is to fit my own interaction rules into Brenda's utterances so that the whole looks like an acceptable question-and-answer sequence.

A few minutes later, Suzanne tries the same approach, but this time Suzanne is actually introducing a new object for Brenda's attention.

(30) (071)   (S) What's this? (Holding up
                                    roll of scotch tape)

          (silence)

                               (C) Don't bother! 'Cause she
                                    not gonna talk. She
                                    doesn't want to.

Charlotte, who was 4;7.6 at the time of this recording and exposed to Brenda much more than Suzanne, understood that Brenda was not likely to respond to this type of questioning.

The only initiating sequence in this tape that resembles later developments is one case where Brenda uses handing plus repetition plus the word *Mommy* to initiate a long conversation with her mother. It is interesting that this elaborate summons of the type that is later used in interaction with visitors only is here used to initiate an interaction with the mother. This, perhaps, indicates the difficulty Brenda experiences in all conversational interactions at this time. In (071) Brenda only sometimes responds to speech with speech. In general she responds to speech with actions and to actions or objects with speech. This agrees with Lewis's (1937) observation that it is at the age of 1;6 that children begin to respond to speech with speech. It further agrees with Halliday's (1973) observation of Phase II (1;6) as the beginning of dialogue.

VI.4.4   Initiations in BRENDA I, Age 1;0.2 to 1;1.22

Since conversations are so rudimentary in this period, there is very little to be said about initiations. In some cases, they simply amount to Brenda calling *Mommy*. In tape (051) the mother's responses to Brenda's utterances are the best indication of the kind of interactions that take place. (This example is quoted in full in VI.1.)

(31) (051)   (M) What's that? Hm? Sausage.
                                  Um. Yum-yum. You want?
                                  That's French fries. You
                                  want? Oh, can't eat from
                                  that. Hm? Oh, yes. That's
                                  for Daddy, yes. Hm? It's
                                  a microphone.

The general pattern for the interchanges between Brenda and her mother is: Brenda says something, (X), the mother says what may be paraphrased as "I take X as Y and Z is how I answer Y." This formula amounts to having the mother carry on both sides of the interaction. Brenda cannot even be said to initiate these interactions since it is the mother who is prompting Brenda to say something with speech, gestures, and objects.

Eight weeks earlier, the interchanges are even more basic. In (012), the mother does not add her answer, Z, to Y but only performs the first part, i.e., "I take X as Y."

(32) (012)12   æp^h (M) Apple? You want apple?
                                  Hm?

The mother tentatively takes Brenda's utterance as being an attempt at apple. But she does not say anything further on the topic. It is fair to say that in BRENDA I Brenda does not engage in conversational interactions.

VI.5 Development and Interactive Ability

Before beginning this study, Brenda's mother had reported to me that at this time Brenda only knew a few words. When I asked her if Brenda responded to things that other people said, she said that Brenda did not, that she "just talks." This assessment is supported by my study of tapes taken at this period. Any speech interaction is of the adult's making and has to be fit in around Brenda's chance utterance. By BRENDA IV, at 2;0.12, Brenda's control over the interactions she engages in is virtually complete. She does not get into interactions she chooses to avoid and controls the topic of the ones she does choose to engage in. She has formal means to do this (although these formal means differ somewhat from the adult means). The report of Brenda's mother that at 1;0.2

Brenda only could say a few words and the later report at 2;0.12 that Brenda "talks a lot now" can be seen to be partly a result of the ease with which Brenda can enter into successful speech interactions.

This raises the "chicken and egg" question: Does Brenda's speech develop because she gains fluency in social control of interactions or vice versa? In tape (17) at 2;0.12, there were cases in which other speaker's exclusion of Brenda as a participant was accompanied by Brenda's speech becoming unintelligible. Does this mean that the lower level of intelligibility/complexity in (141) or (071) or (012) is because Brenda fails first to establish an active participant role? Or does she fail to establish this role because of a fundamental unintelligibility of her speech to others?

I think the answer is that both things happen. For any "period," someone speaking to Brenda sizes up her ability to talk. This, then, determines that speaker's expectations for her in interactions and in that sense limits what they will allow Brenda to do. In the case of the mother or another caretaker where there is frequent opportunity to re-evaluate this sizing-up, Brenda is probably allowed maximum flexibility.

This sizing-up undoubtedly goes both ways. I think Brenda knows who can understand her and who cannot. In the case of visitors, her working assumption seems to be that they will not understand her. After a visitor has said a series of successful utterances (utterances where Brenda has understood him), he is finally allowed to engage in full interaction with Brenda.

VI.6   Adult Speech

In order to assess the amount of adjustment adults make in speaking to Brenda, I have calculated the mean length of utterance (MLU) for two adults, the mother and myself, both in interaction with Brenda and with the other speakers. The data are taken from a tape for an early session (041) and again for the latest session (171) recorded. I have also counted up questions and declaratives/imperatives. Finally, I have figured the percentages of the total speech directed to either Brenda or the others. The figures that indicate a type of "baby talk" shifting are given in Table 15. Table 16 illustrates these figures with graphs. Of course, they will need considerable explanation.

TABLE 15. Adult Speech

	Mother		Investigator	
	to Brenda	to Others	to Brenda	to Others
Adult MLU[a]				
(041)[b]	1.78	5.52	3.57	6.48
(171)[c]	3.13	5.08	3.29	5.48
Percent of total speech				
(041)	87.9	12.1	67.4	32.6
(171)	66.2	33.8	85.3	14.7
Questions as percent of total speech[d]				
(041)	39.8	15.5	46.0	16.7
(171)	34.0	20.8	42.7	35.0

[a] MLU—Mean Length of Utterance.
[b] (041)—Age 1;1.8, MLU 1.0.
[c] (171)—Age 2;0.12, MLU 2.29.
[d] Remaining speech made up of declaratives and imperatives.

I should say first that statistics of this sort are only general indicators and should not be taken too seriously. There is also a problem of the sample size. I have used Brown's (1973, p. 66) rules for tabulating MLU's. However, in the case of any speech but that of young children, the MLU is highly inaccurate, as Brown points out. Further, in the case of speech between adults there was never a full set of 100 utterances on any one tape. The MLU's for adults to adults have been calculated on a smaller set, that is, whatever happened to occur in that tape.

The figures on questions have been derived by counting question marks. Of course, this does not indicate sentences that have a declarative form but a question intent.

The percentages of speech have been figures on the total that appeared on the half-hour tape under consideration. In spite of the highly tentative nature of these statistics, I feel that they are striking enough to give a broad indication of several interesting phenomena.

In the first part of Tables 15 and 16, the MLU's are given. Comparing the mother's MLU in speech to Brenda with Brenda's MLU at that time, we can see a clear "development" of the mother's speech. In (041) it averages .78 morphemes longer than Brenda's. In (171) it averages .84 morphemes longer. It appears that the mother is successively retracting her extended system as Brenda develops. That this does not represent a general development on the part of the mother can be seen from the fact that her speech to others remains relatively constant.

In the case of my own speech, an interesting fact emerges. In the first place, as the study progresses there is a reverse development in my speech to Brenda. At the time of (041), although my speech to Brenda is simplified in comparison with my speech to others, it did not reach the extreme the mother achieved. With time, however, my system in interaction with Brenda eventually became very similar to the mother's. A second interesting fact is that my speech to others also shows a reduction in overall length. This was an amazing observation to me since, in spite of the fact that I was transcribing my own speech from week to week, I was unaware of any change. Perhaps it may be accounted for by the fact that the mother's Japanese Hawaiian English has a number of features which have the net result of a shorter MLU than for Standard English. In the course of these taping sessions, I had effectively varied my Standard English to approximate the Hawaiian English of the home.

The second set of figures in Tables 15 and 16 indicates that in both sessions under consideration the mother and I used many more questions in speaking to Brenda than to others, although in both sessions I used more questions than the mother.

The final set of figures in Tables 15 and 16 indicates reversal in the amount of speech to Brenda between the mother and me during these sessions. In the early session a large percentage (87.9 percent) of the mother's total speech is directed to the child. In the last session only 66.2 percent is addressed to Brenda. In the first session I addressed 67.4 percent of my speech to Brenda, and in the last session it was 85.4 percent. Both of us, however, addressed more speech to Brenda than to others.

TABLE 16.1. Adult Speech—Mean Length of Utterance (MLU)

```
        (041)                                    (171)

MLU                             MLU

 7 ┌──────────────────────┐      7 ┌──────────────────────────┐
   │                to O  │        │                          │
   │                 III  │        │                          │
 6 ┤                 III  │      6 ┤                          │
   │         to O    III  │        │                    to O  │
   │         MMM     III  │        │             to O    III  │
 5 ┤         MMM     III  │      5 ┤             MMM     III  │
   │         MMM     III  │        │             MMM     III  │
   │         MMM     III  │        │             MMM     III  │
 4 ┤         MMM     III  │      4 ┤             MMM     III  │
   │         MMM to B III │        │      to B   MMM to B III │
   │         MMM III III  │        │   MMM MMM   III     III  │
 3 ┤         MMM III III  │      3 ┤   MMM MMM   III     III  │
   │         MMM III III  │        │   MMM MMM   III     III  │
   │         MMM III III  │        │   MMM MMM   III     III  │
 2 ┤         MMM III III  │      2 ┤ BBB MMM MMM III     III  │
   │  to B   MMM III III  │        │ BBB MMM MMM III     III  │
   │     MMM MMM III III  │        │ BBB MMM MMM III     III  │
 1 ┤     MMM MMM III III  │      1 ┤ BBB MMM MMM III     III  │
   │ BBB MMM MMM III III  │        │ BBB MMM MMM III     III  │
   │ BBB MMM MMM III III  │        │ BBB MMM MMM III     III  │
 0 └ BBB MMM MMM III III ─┘      0 └ BBB MMM MMM III     III ─┘
```

TABLE 16.2. Adult Speech—Questions and Declaratives/Imperatives (percent of total speech)

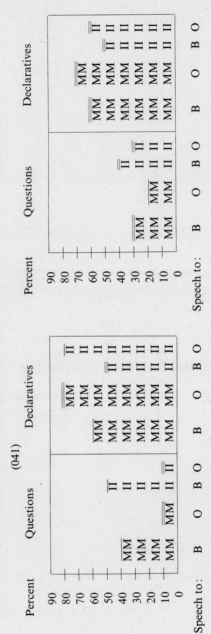

TABLE 16.3. Adult Speech—Percent of Total Speech

Speech to: B   O   B   O

B—Brenda; O—Others; II—Investigator's speech; MM—Mother's speech; BBB—MLU for Brenda; III—MLU for Investigator; MMM—MLU for Mother.

VI.7   **The Cultural Concept "Being Able to Talk"**

This discussion of Brenda's interactive ability and the adults' speech to her suggests two interesting and apparently conflicting facts. The first is that as Brenda grows older she pays closer attention to speech directed to her, filtering out peripheral speech. The second is that the younger Brenda is the more focused the speech to her is by means of baby talk shifts. On the surface it looks as if the cultural wisdom embodied in baby talk is largely wasted. This is only true if the reason for using baby talk is to make it easier for the baby to understand. That position is hard to support in the face of evidence of baby talk to a three-day-old infant (Scollon 1974) or the use of this register to small animals. If baby talk is used to communicate about social/language role, however, this focus is not wasted. We have anecdotes at least to support that children can observe that their speech is different from adults' speech (and many explanations for why this should be so). I suggest that what baby talk tells the child is what amount and what kinds of difference are acceptable.

It does this in two ways. The first way is by simple modeling. By showing the child both full adult careful forms (overheard as well as directed to the child) and the reduced and otherwise altered forms of baby talk, one is displaying for the child a cultural theory of the language. This modeling says, in effect: This is the kind of difference expected or possible in our language.

I do not mean to suggest that I think the way a baby talks is the same as the way adults talk to babies. I only mean that baby talk encodes the wisdom of the language about possible range of variation. It is not necessary for adults to always talk baby talk to children. In fact that would fail to demonstrate variability. The optimal model is one that ranges from the most careful and normative forms of the adult speech to the most marked forms of baby talk.

The second way baby talk tells the child what is acceptable is by telling the child about her role in cultural life. I think the data I have presented here show that Brenda at two years was aware of some interactive roles and some rules governing them. I suggest that baby talk has functioned to indicate to Brenda her interactive role and in doing so has provided the pressure to adopt a different role with increasing age. The way baby talk communicates this role pressure is by telling Brenda what degrees of variability are permissible.

SECTION III

Construction:
Horizontal and Vertical

CHAPTER VII

Types of Construction

VII.1   The History of this Study

I have said several times that at the beginning of this study and for most of the time I was collecting the tapes on which it is based I thought of it as a study of phonology and intonation during the one-word period. At the end of BRENDA II, I still thought that phonology was my primary interest. During the last tape (141), age 1;8.21, Brenda said several things that I took as two-word constructions, and on the basis of those I terminated BRENDA II.

Three of these constructions were striking. In the first, Brenda lifted her foot over my tape recorder and while she pretended to step on it said,

(1)   (141)27   tape
          28   step

In the second case she reached out with her index finger and delicately touched the microphone saying,

(2)   (141)139   finger
          140   touch

Later, while I was turning the pages of a book we were "reading," Brenda looked at a picture of a woman who was cooking at a stove and said,

    (3)　(141)201　cook
            202　say

I was surprised by this and said, "What'd the cook say?" Brenda's answer was "something."

    At the time of making the transcription for this tape (141), however, I did not transcribe the utterances above exactly as they are shown. First, I transcribed them phonetically. Second, I transcribed them on one line of the transcription, which indicated to me that they were all of the same utterance. My ambivalence about their status as utterances is clear, though, from the fact that I gave each part its own utterance number. The reason for my vacillation was that these utterances appeared to be connected in every way but intonation contour. At the time, these utterances and the others like them convinced me that Brenda was either beginning or very nearly beginning the two-word stage.

    In the two months that followed, I did not take any new recordings. During this time I began the work on which Section II of this presentation is based. In doing that work, I kept finding cases in which Brenda appeared to be trying to put several words together in a longer construction. One example of this was quoted in part in the study of phonology, as well as in the introduction (I.1). On tape (071) when Brenda was 1;7.2 she held up her mother's shoe and, while she stared directly at it, she said,

    (4)　(071)259　mama
            260　mama
            261　mama
            262　mam
            263　š
            264　šɪ
            265　š
            266　šɪš
            267　šu
            268　šuʔ
            269　šuš

                          (S)　Shoes!
            270　ši
            271　ši
            272　šuʔ

There are several pieces of evidence that indicate that Brenda is making some kind of construction here. The first is that without any intervention from another speaker she goes from the first word, *mama*, to the second, *shoe*. The second indication that she is really trying to say something is her persistence. In spite of rather formidable production difficulties, Brenda persists until a recognizable surface form of each word is performed.

A second example of this sort of construction has been presented in the phonology chapter (III.9). In the case of *tall . . . clown*, I pointed out that either of these words when produced independently caused no difficulty in performance. However, when produced together as a construction there were a number of unintelligible but apparently related forms.

In looking again at the constructions of tape (141), I noticed the same phenomenon. In most of these, when the words appeared separately there was a form that was altered in some way when used in construction. Several examples will illustrate this alteration. The words *tape* and *step* both appear independently on (141). The phonetic shape of *tape* is [tʰeip]; *step* is [tɛpʰ]. When the two occur together, however, the phonetic shape is [tʰei.tɛʔ]. The final consonant of *tape* disappears, and the final consonant of *step* is reduced to [ʔ]. These changes can be seen as simplifications in the sense that they have been characteristic at an earlier stage of phonological development. That is, at an earlier stage these same words occurred without final consonants or with just [ʔ].

In the case of *finger.touch.*, something similar happens, except that neither of these words occurs separately on this tape. In the analysis of Brenda's phonology for this tape, I have concluded that there is a clear distinction between [pʰ] and [f]. For example, there are [pʰido] *Peter* and [pʰĩ] *pink* for [pʰ], and [fwai] *fly* and [faĩŋ] *flying* for [f]. Developmentally the [pʰ] represents an earlier stage in places where the adult has [f]. In this construction, *finger. touch.*, the phonetic shape is [pʰiŋgə.tʰəč]. It appears that here is another example of the phonetic shape being reduced in some way to a less complex form with the addition of the complexity of construction. (See VIII.4 for a discussion of another type of restriction in complexity.)

As a final example, in *read.page.* [ritʰ.peč] the initial consonant of *page* is the unaspirated [p], and in *pink car* [pʰĩka] the initial consonant of car is [k].

At first, these constructions arose as problems in phonology. I was concerned with determining the "good" form and separating out the forms that appeared to be suffering from performance limitations. In these cases, however, the performance limitation could be described as the presence of the word in a larger construction. It was that larger construction that I found I had no means of describing. This study is the result of trying to make explicit the types of construction in which intonationally separate utterances fit.

To continue the narrative, I was still puzzling over problems of this sort when I recorded Brenda at age 1;10.17, tape (161–162). On this tape, which is the only data of BRENDA III, I found two-word sentences in abundance. In making the transcription, I found that it was quite easy to distinguish these sentences from the earlier constructions I had been thinking about. In making the transcription, I wrote them together on one line and gave them one utterance number. I then decided that the earlier constructions should not be classed together with these sentences since there were clearly two types of construction. This was the point at which I coined the terms "horizontal" and "vertical" constructions. The terminology came out of the format of my transcription with horizontal constructions being those sequences of two words that I grouped under one utterance number and vertical constructions being those sequences of two words that I grouped under separate utterance numbers.

VII.2   Horizontal Construction in BRENDA II

It was an accident of the layout of transcription that supplied both terminology and conceptual foundation for my thinking about constructions. I call sentences horizontal constructions, and I call the other ones, for which the tradition had not given me a name, vertical constructions. In the first case, then, I have avoided using such terms as "sentence," "pivot-open," "telegraphic," and "two-word." In the second case, I have invented a term that expresses the constructional nature of the utterances while keeping them separate from horizontal constructions.

Brown and Bellugi-Klima (1964, 1971, p. 307) made explicit the criterion for determining what I call horizontal constructions: When two words (or morphemes) are grouped together under the same primary stress terminal intonation contour they constitute a single utterance. In the terms of this study, primary stress and terminal intonation contour are represented by FX intonation. Two more criteria can be mentioned, although they will have to be modified later. The first is the pause between the two morphemes. In horizontal constructions in BRENDA II, there were no pauses greater than $\frac{3}{5}$ second. For the most part, the pauses were even shorter. It should be noted that pauses of $\frac{3}{5}$ second and under are difficult to time with any accuracy using a hand-held stopwatch. The meaning of these preceding statements, then, is that the pauses in horizontal constructions were too short to be timed accurately. In vertical constructions there was some variation ranging from one second to as much as eight seconds. These pauses which are more susceptible to being timed will be specified more clearly in the following discussion of vertical construction (VII.4). The point I am making here is that for horizontal construction the pause is minimal and can be clearly distinguished from that of vertical construction.

The other criterion that can be mentioned is that each of the morphemes must show independence. If no independence can be demonstrated, it is likely that the utterance in question is what might be called an idiom rather than a construction. That is, the child has simply memorized the whole without constructing it from its parts.

With these three criteria in mind for horizontal constructions, I want to review the data of BRENDA II. Table 17 is a selection of various constructions found in BRENDA II. There are many more. It is difficult, however, to say how many more since in addition to clear cases there are cases in which one or more but not all of the criteria are met. Of these constructions, only E5, E10, and E21 appear to be horizontal. The earliest, E5, is from (071) age 1;7.2. Just what it was intended to mean is difficult to say. It might consist of *swim* and *boat*. It does meet the three criteria to the limited extent that it is intelligible. I think it is best to consider this utterance marginal at most.

E10 and E21, *hot water* and *pink car*, are both said with the primary stress terminal contour pattern. Both have a very short pause between them (under $\frac{3}{5}$ second). In both cases the two words have been used independently in these and other sessions, which is a strong indication that they are true horizontal constructions. Of course, it is plausible that Brenda could have learned not

TABLE 17. Constructions from BRENDA II

Example	Tape	Utterance	(Repetitions)	Input Speech
E1	(071)63–65	net	(3x)	
	66	you do	(2x)	
	67–71	net	(5x)	
	72	you do	(2x)	
E2	(071)250–253	Mommy	(4x)	(pulling things out
	254, 255	hankie	(2x)	of M's closet)
E3	(071)259–262	Mama	(4x)	
	263–269	[š] . . . shoes	(7x)	
				(S) Shoes!
	270–272	[š] . . . shoe	(3x)	
E4	(071)277	Mama		
	278–282	shoe	(5x)	
E5	(071)307–309	boat	(3x)	
	310–312	s . . . swim	(3x)	
				(M) Swim, yeah.
	313–315	boat	(3x)	
				Boat swims, yeah.
	316–318	boat	(3x)	
	319	[swɛʔəbəutʸ]	(1x)	
	320	boat		
E6	(091)77–79	tall	(3x)	
	80	Brenda		
	81–	tall		
	86	clown		(Note that although there are four utterances between 81 and 86 it is impossible to determine which are *tall* and which are *clown*— see III.9)
	87–90	tall	(4x)	
	91	girl		
	92–96	clown	(5x)	
	97, 98	tall	(2x)	

TABLE 17—*Continued*

Example	Tape	Utterance	(*Repetitions*)		Input Speech
E7	(121)49	Brenda			
	50	sleeping			
E8	(121)67	Kimby			
				(M)	What about Kimby?
	68	close			
E9	(121)120	Brenda			
				(M)	Oh, Brenda?
	121–123	ate	(3x)		
	124	eating			
E10	(131)16–21	hot water	(6x)		
	22	hot			
E11	(141)2	hiding			
				(R)	Hide? What's hiding?
	3	balloon			
E12	(141)18–20	Ron	(3x)		
				(R)	What?
	21–25	carry	(5x)		
E13	(141)27	tape			
	28	step			
E14	(141)43–45	dere	(3x)		
	46–49	black	(4x)		
E15	(141)129	bump me [bəm:pʰ:mi]			
E16	(141)139	finger			
	140	touch			
E17	(141)158	read			
	159	page			

Tᴀʙʟᴇ 17—*Continued*

Example	Tape	Utterance	(Repetitions)		Input Speech
E18	(141)201	cook			
	202	say			
				(R)	Hm? (S) The cook said.
				(R)	What'd the cook say?
	203	something			
E19	(141)231	please			
	232	read			
E20	(141)253	owl			
	254, 255	flying	(2x)		
E21	(141)291, 292	car	(2x)		
	293, 294	pink car	(2x)		
	295	pink			

only the free forms *hot, water, pink, car* but also the "constructed" forms *hot water* and *pink car*. I think that *hot water* is most likely learned as a whole, particularly considering that in the mother's Japanese *hot water* is a single morpheme, *oyu*, and that on occasion she uses this word with the children.

The case of *pink car* is interesting since it does not occur just as that but rather as a type of build-up. To repeat the example, it is *car . car . pink car . pink car . pink*. This example appears to present the strongest case for horizontal construction in the data of BRENDA II. Curiously enough, it occurs within ten minutes of the end of the last tape (141).

VII.3 Vertical Construction in BRENDA II

The constructional nature of horizontal constructions has been well established in the literature (Braine 1963, 1971; Brown and Bellugi-Klima 1964, 1971; Miller and Ervin 1964, 1971), although the structural meaning is far from settled (Bloom 1970; Bowerman

1973; Brown 1973). I am going to assume that the reader accepts that horizontal constructions are genuine constructions and shall talk mostly about vertical constructions. To call something a construction we need some evidence that it did not happen that way by accident. To link two or more utterances that are not linked by an intonational pattern, other evidence has to be considered.

I can describe four types of vertical construction in BRENDA II, which I shall call types A, B, C and D, in the order of the strength of the intentional linkage, type A being the most obvious construction and type D being the weakest case. These types of constructions and the evidence for them will now be discussed.

VII.3.1   Type A Vertical Construction

Type A, which is the last to develop, is very similar to horizontal construction. It consists of two one-word utterances in close succession with silence before and after. The words are linked in construction but not in intonational contour. By "linked" I mean that there is a definite semantic connection between the words that is appropriate to the context. Further, these separate words taken together perform a single speech act. The constructions of this type are almost all found in (141). Example E7 of Table 17 is the only instance of type A vertical construction that is found earlier than the last session. The others are E13, E15, E17, E18, and E19. In E13, *tape.step*, the word order is the opposite of that expected on the basis of the ordering of horizontal constructions (see Chapter 8). Apparently, word order in vertical construction is considerably more flexible than in horizontal construction. Since these constructions are so much like horizontal constructions, I think it is likely that they have been grouped together in some of the reported studies as "two-word" constructions. That would account for some of the earlier despair found, particularly in diary studies, over the lack of regular word ordering. (See for example Velten 1943, 1971, p. 89 who claims that syntax "begins with complete anarchy.")

VII.3.2   Type B Vertical Construction

The second type of vertical construction, type B, which appears much earlier than type A, is like type A in that two words occur in sequence that show an appropriate semantic connection and perform a single speech act. These two types differ only in that in type B either word or both words may be repeated. The example quoted earlier of *mama . . . shoe* is of this type. It is clear from the context that Brenda is making the statement, "This is Mama's shoe." This is evidenced by the fact that after finally saying *mama* to her satisfaction she moves on to the second word. I have also pointed out the difficulty with which she does this. These two kinds of evidence indicate that she is making a construction.

In these two types of construction, types A and B, it is clear that Brenda is trying to say something beyond the limits of a single-word utterance. It should be pointed out now that these two types are on a developmental continuum. What I mean is that the examples of type A are almost all found in the last session (141), whereas the type B constructions are found throughout the earlier sessions of BRENDA II.

Table 17 gives eight examples of type B vertical constructions: E1, E2, E3, E4, E5, E6, E14, and E20. From these examples and from the earlier discussion of phonological alterations in constructions, it can be seen that the development of type B can be measured in terms of difficulty. First the difficulty shows up in the great number of repetitions and in the phonetic instability of the words used in construction. As Brenda's phonology and construction ability improve, there are fewer repetitions and great stability in phonetic shape. Ultimately, type B becomes type A when no repetition of the separate elements is necessary. Then the only indication of difficulty is that the phonetic shape suffers.

VII.3.3   Type C Vertical Construction

Existing parallel to these two types of construction are two others that are not radically different. Type C constructions are like type A in that two words are linked semantically and without repetition. However, in these constructions the speech of another speaker intervenes. The second part of (3) above (VII.1) is of this type. Brenda says, *something* in response to my asking, "What'd the cook say?" Whether or not her *something* should be understood to be in direct linkage with her earlier two words is difficult to say. It is certainly appropriate to my question. But, in turn, my question had the effect of asking for a constituent to fill out Brenda's construction.

Table 17 gives three examples of this type of construction: E8, E9, and E11. In E8 the mother could not make sense from Brenda's utterance and simply asked her, "What about Kimby?" The case of E11 is similar. In both examples the other speakers have apparently taken Brenda's first utterance as the statement of a topic and have asked her to clarify it or comment on it. From the point of view of topic-comment construction, the apparent lack of word order in vertical construction is not so disquieting. E13 (*tape.step.*), mentioned above, could well be described as a topic-comment construction.

The topic-comment type of structure is fairly common in the Hawaiian English of Brenda's father (Odo 1973). For example, he says "Diplomat that" (with "tag" or "defocused" intonation on *that*) in a context where Standard English would have something like *A real diplomat is what he is*. This indicates that for at least a part of Brenda's speech environment, topic-comment construction represents a mature form. But rather than belabor the topic-comment point, I want to suggest here that this interaction with other speakers, as in these examples of type C constructions, may well be the means by which Brenda has learned how to construct in the first place.

VII.3.4   Type D Vertical Construction

As more evidence that interaction with other speakers is crucial to the development of vertical construction, we can look at the fourth, and by far most common type, type D. These constructions amount to a combination of types B and C. That is, any of the words may be repeated and there is the intervention of other speakers. The tapes are literally full of interactions of this type. Some of them have rather shaky status as constructions in that the words appear to be simply the listing of separate elements of an object or a situation or, perhaps, a listing of a group of attributes. However, in many of these constructions (one of which is repeated from V.6.2) it is evident that Brenda intended to go on to the second word but was simply waiting for verification from the listener that he had understood.

(5)   (111)1   fĕĩ   (B is looking at electric fan)
         2   fǽ

           (M)   Hm?

3 fæ̃

Bathroom?

4 fanĩ
5 faĩ

Fan! Yeah.

6 kʰu

Cool, yeah. Fan makes you
cool.

In the case of types A and B, I described them as being on a
continuum, with type A as the final development. The same can be
said of types C and D, but with some qualification. As Brenda's
phonology improves, and as the adults' understanding improves,
the number of repetitions needed to get a response decreases. Again,
examples of type C tend to be found in the later sessions, and
examples of type D are found more frequently in the earlier sessions.
The qualification that must be added is that there is really no clear
distinction between vertical constructions in which another speaker
intervenes and those in which there is no intervention. In many
cases, the intervention is simply an accidental simultaneity and
no relation can be established. In many other cases, there is a clear
relation between what the other speaker says after Brenda's topic
and what Brenda says in comment. But in some of these cases, at
least, it is not clear that she would not have said the same thing
anyway. Finally, in other cases it is clear that Brenda is only waiting
for some indication that her first utterance was within some tolerance
limits of understanding, after which she gets on with the construction.

VII.3.5   Relationship Between the Four Types of Vertical Construction

Perhaps a diagram of these four types of vertical construction
will be helpful. The four types can be cross-classified on the dimensions of repetition and intervening discourse ("interlocution"). The
following diagram indicates this cross-classification.

(6)

	without interlocution	with interlocution
without repetition	A	C
with repetition	B	D

Remember that the elimination of repetition in the production of vertical constructions is a later development. The freedom from dependency on interaction with another speaker is also a later development. These two facts operate to make the other types of construction eventually converge on type A as the culmination of a developmental trend.

VII.4   The Three Criteria for Construction

Now we can review vertical construction in general from the point of view of the three criteria for horizontal construction listed above (VII.2). The first criterion was that the two morphemes be grouped under one sentence intonation contour. In vertical construction, each separate morpheme is given this pattern. They are separated from horizontal constructions by this criterion.

The second criterion is that there is either a short pause (under $\frac{3}{5}$ second) or no pause between the two morphemes. In the selected vertical constructions of Table 17, the pauses are longer. In type A there is a range from one second (just one case) to $2\frac{2}{5}$ seconds (three cases). Type B varied from one second (one case) to $8\frac{2}{5}$ seconds (also one case) between the last token of the first series and the first token of the second series. Normally the pauses in type B were less than $3\frac{1}{5}$ seconds. Type C varied from $2\frac{2}{5}$ to $4\frac{2}{5}$ seconds. Type D constructions stayed within these ranges but were more variable.

Since these time lapses are somewhat inaccurately timed, I think it is better to generalize by saying that for a construction to be classed as horizontal it must have a pause of less than $\frac{3}{5}$ seconds, the lower threshold for timing. When the pause is between one and four seconds, a sequence is likely to be a vertical construction. When the pause is longer, the constructional status becomes questionable.

The third criterion, that the separate morphemes occur independently, is somewhat strained in this context of vertical construction, since the other two criteria define the morphemes of a vertical construction as separate utterances to begin with. However, in many cases, such as *tall* and *clown*, these words were used independently, as well as in the vertical construction. Their independence could be judged more or less objectively by the phonological stability of the forms.

There are several things that must be clarified about these

criteria. In the first place, it should be remembered that they have been applied *after* making the judgment about the constructional nature of the utterances in question. That is, they are not the means of determining horizontal constructions but rather an attempt to make explicit the intuitions of the investigator who made the initial judgment. In reapplying these criteria to vertical construction, I am making explicit the intuitions by which I have decided about these constructions.

From this it should be evident that these are not the only criteria that have been called into play in deciding about constructions. There is a fourth and very important criterion that I have had to use. That is the criterion that the constructions have to "make sense" as constructions. To my knowledge, this criterion has never been made explicit in previous discussions in the literature. It is, however, at the foundation of all the studies of early constructions. It is assumed that whatever is grouped together as a horizontal construction (that can be recognized by an adult as a horizontal construction) will make sense as a construction. I am arguing that this amounts to a fourth criterion that has been used for constructions. And I further argue that since it has been applied to horizontal construction, it should also be applied to vertical construction. It is this criterion that I am appealing to when I say above that when "two words occur in sequence that show an appropriate semantic connection" they are in vertical construction. It is because of my ultimate reliance on my own intuitions and my appeal to the reader's intuitions that I have ordered these four types of vertical construction "in the order of the strength of this intentional linkage, type A being the most obvious construction and type D being the weakest case."

VII.5   Vertical Construction in BRENDA I

In outlining the history of my understanding of vertical construction, I said that at first I heard the vertical constructions of type A in tape (141) as horizontal constructions. It was only while making the transcription of (161–162), in which horizontal constructions appeared in abundance, that I realized that these earlier constructions were not the same. This led first to a re-examination of the constructions on tape (141). That, in turn, led to a re-examination of the full set of tapes that I have called BRENDA II (age

1;7.2 to 1;8.21). The result of that study was the classification of the four types discussed above.

Then it occurred to me that I might be able to find evidence for the beginnings of this construction even as early as BRENDA I. The earliest sequence of utterances that looks anything like this was in tape (031) when Brenda was 1;0.23. The situation is as follows:

(7)	(031)	(B is seated at the table in her high chair. C's broken doll is on the table in front of B)
	(M)	What is that?
		What is that?
		What is that?
53	a:la	
		What? Hm? What's that, Brenda?
	(F)	What's that?
	(M)	What's that?
54	dau	

The utterance 53 is an acceptable form of *Charlotte* for that period. Utterance 54 is *doll*. If we were to look only at this sequence of utterances, ignoring the adult speech, it would look like a type A construction, *Charlotte.doll*. And it was, in fact, Charlotte's doll. I am not going to suggest that Brenda has made this construction. What is interesting to me is how the interaction of the parents' repeated prompting and Brenda's own ideas had the cumulative effect of producing this sequence. For this reason, I suggest that early interactions of this type might well provide the foundation on which the vertical constructions that come later in this period and, ultimately, horizontal constructions are built.

Three weeks later on tape (051), Brenda was reaching for Suzanne's necklace. She said:

(8)	(051)6	nene
	7	nene
	8	avau

On the basis of decisions made about Brenda's phonology for this period, we can say that she says two words here: ⟨nene⟩

('nurture') and ⟨awəu⟩ ('I want'). The time lapse between 6 and 7 is $2\frac{1}{5}$ seconds; between 7 and 8 it is $1\frac{4}{5}$ seconds. It looks very much like a type B vertical construction. The problem is that it doesn't seem to mean anything.

Before discussing this in detail, three more examples from the same tape will be given and then discussed together.

(9) (051)   (Looking at food in picture
                                  magazine)
                                  (M)   Manman, uh huh.
        58   məmæ
        59   mɛmæ
                                  (M)   Yeah.
        60   ava
                                  (M)   You want? Oh, can't eat
                                        from that.
(10) (051)   (B picks up Daddy's magazine)
        61   dædi
        62   awau
                                  (M)   Hm? Oh, yes. That's for
                                        Daddy. Yes x x x for
                                        Daddy.
(11) (051)89 na   (B empties juice from cup)
                                  (R)   What?
        90   nau
                                  (R)   Now? No?
        91   aweu
                                  (S)   Allgone. [sic]
        92   æwã

In (9) the first word ⟨mæmə⟩ ('solid food') is prompted by the mother. However, the ⟨awəu⟩ is spontaneous and taken by the mother to mean that Brenda wants the food she sees. That is, the mother takes the first word (or the picture) as a topic and the second word as a comment on that topic.

In (10) the meaning of the second word is not easily determined, but the meaning of the whole is taken again as some sort of comment on the magazine, not as an error of calling it by the wrong name. The same is true of (11) where, although there is no clear understanding on the part of the adults of what Brenda is saying, there is an understanding of the whole. That is, the cup is empty and Brenda wants more.

It should be seen from these four examples that they represent a very rudimentary sort of construction. In each case one of the words ⟨nau⟩, ⟨dædi⟩, or ⟨mæmə⟩ was placed in position before ⟨awəu⟩. It should be remembered that in the study of the phonology of this session these words represent the great majority of the words used at this time. Apparently, the meaning of this construction is similar to that of a topic-comment construction. That is to say that first some object is mentioned by name and then commented on. It may be true that the best meaning for ⟨awəu⟩ is just that—'comment'. In some cases, it is likely that the comment is suggested by the interaction as in type C and D vertical constructions.

The tentative nature of these constructions is seen in two ways. The first indication is that they are quite rare. It would be very risky to attribute too much generality to a phenomenon that only occurred six times in BRENDA I. The second indication is that most of these constructions consist of some word plus ⟨awəu⟩. This word, although very frequent in (051) and again in (052), (061) and (S11), has completely disappeared by BRENDA II, four months later.

VII.6 Summary of Vertical Construction in the One-Word Period: BRENDA I and BRENDA II

Let us review the general development of vertical construction in the putative one-word period. It begins with highly tentative constructions in discourse that are cluttered with misunderstanding, repetitions, phonological distortions, and other indicators of difficulty. With development, all of these problems are reduced. Other speakers respond to Brenda more frequently as her phonological control becomes more secure. This has the effect of requiring fewer repetitions to achieve the same end. Finally, Brenda arrives at the point where she can put two words together in sequence with only a distortion of phonetic shape and, perhaps, word order difficulty, although word order is generally consistent with later horizontal construction. She has arrived at the threshold of horizontal construction, not by miracle nor by accident, but by a fairly long process of active practice of construction in social interaction within her community.

VII.7   Construction in BRENDA III

I have said that my interest in the vertical construction of BRENDA II came out of a contrast of those constructions with the horizontal constructions in tape (161–162) at age 1;10.17. During the time that I was working out the developments described above, I continued looking at the horizontal constructions of BRENDA III.

VII.7.1   Horizontal Construction in BRENDA III

I have described the four criteria that are used in determining horizontal constructions: intonation contour, a pause under $\frac{3}{5}$ seconds between the two morphemes, the independence of the two morphemes, and a semantically appropriate link between them. The first criterion, intonation contour, can stand without qualification, but the others need to be discussed.

The second criterion for horizontal construction is that the elements are not separated by a significant time lapse. In BRENDA II the few horizontal constructions that were suggested had a lapse of $\frac{3}{5}$ second or less between the separate element. For the horizontal constructions of Table 18, $\frac{3}{5}$ second is certainly a maximum, but for the most part there is no lapse at all but rather noticeable transitional features from one morpheme or constituent to the next.

Table 18 lists all of the horizontal constructions of (161–162). In many of the examples listed, we can see that the words used also appear in Appendix B. That is, they are words that have been used independently in BRENDA II. In some cases, however, it is not true that they can be found earlier. For example, *wash* does not occur in BRENDA II. It does appear in (162). The full section on which *wash clothing* and *wash clothes* appear is as follows:

(12)   (162)93   wash clothing
            94   wash
            95   wash
            96   wash
            97   wash clothes
            98   wash clothes

As (12) shows, the word may not have actually appeared

TABLE 18. Horizontal Constructions in BRENDA III

Group 1	*found it	Group 5
[a]*Ron talk	have it	who dere
*Brenda talk	stick it	Brenda here
*corder talk	scrub it	water on it
*cat sleeping	clean it	
*monster go	dry it	Group 6
*monster eat	drain it	*in there
Brenda read now	write it	on dere
*more coming out	*bring it	
Peach Boy coming out	*bend it	Group 7
		icy juicy
Group 2	Group 3	*my turn
*see that	*picture mark	*scary monster
eat this	key lock	*banana leaf
*read dat		horsie-ride
*like that	Group 4	paper napkin
*like that song	*bring home	
*see Ron	*bring it home	Group 8
*drink soup	*take home	*dat one cat
*wash clothing	*take it home	*dis cat
*wash clothes	fill up	*this way
*hiding Halet[b]	fill it up	*this is way
*hiding Brenda	fill up it	
lock it	*cut it down	Group 9
read it	*tree down	*dog some
now read it	*horn off	*doggie some
*do it	leave it on	
*use it	*put it on	Group 10
pick it	get out	thank you
wind it	get up	don't Halet[b]
*hold it	*turning around	
find it	gassing up	

[a] An asterisk (*) indicates that a construction formed part of a larger construction. See Table 20.
[b] Halet is *Charlotte*

earlier or separately in my sample, but at the time it does show a certain amount of independence.

A different item that is more difficult to explain is the *it* that appears in many constructions. This *it* is definitely not used as a separate morpheme here or elsewhere. In VIII.4 some evidence will be given that this *it*, rather than being the adult pronoun *it*, is more like a dummy symbol or perhaps in some cases a transitivizing particle, that is, an inflection on the verb. Whatever its status may be, it will cause us to broaden somewhat the criterion that each word or morpheme in a horizontal construction must be used independently elsewhere before the whole will be accepted as a construction.

A second type of apparent exception in Table 18 will be taken up before returning to the broader criterion. Notice *more coming out* and *Peach Boy coming out*. These two examples raise the question of what is a word or morpheme for Brenda. *More* has been used independently for some time. *Coming out* is new on this tape. *Peach Boy* is an English version of *Momotaro* from the Japanese story of that name. It might legitimately be considered a single word. Since BRENDA II, however, she has used the word *boy* independently. Apparently *Peach Boy* and *boy* are similar to *hot water* and *hot* as discussed in BRENDA II (VII.2). That is, for Brenda they are two separate words, the relationship between them as adults see it being nonexistent for her.

From these two types of apparent exception to the "two-word" criterion, we can see that it might, perhaps, be more accurate to speak of two constituents. By using "constituent," such a dependent form as *it* as well as such apparently complex forms as *coming out* can be treated as a single element in a two-element construction. In a two-constituent construction, however, at least one of the constituents must occur independently.

As far as the fourth criterion is concerned, a look at the horizontal constructions in Table 18 will show that these constructions are quite similar to those described by other investigators. (For earlier studies see Braine 1963, 1971; Miller and Ervin 1964, 1971. For a recent review of the field see Bloom 1970; Bowerman 1973; or especially Brown 1973.) The discussion of the internal structure of constructions that is the basis for this fourth criterion is taken up in Chapter 8.

The mean length of utterance (MLU) for (161–162) is 1.46 (See II.2.2.7 for clarification). Based on this measure, Brenda can be seen to be in the very middle of what Brown has labelled Stage I, MLU 1.0–MLU 2.0 (Brown 1973). Among the misrepresentations of this stage, perhaps the most glaring is expressed by Dale (1972, p. 40) when he refers to "two-word utterances" (horizontal, not vertical as "the most common type of language at this stage." Table 19 gives a count of the one-word and two-word utterances (tokens) for (161) and a selected count for (162). Looking first at (161), we can see that the two-word utterances account for only 22.1 percent of the total. One-word utterances are 53.4 percent of the total. Of the 22.1 percent that are unintelligible but were transcribed, nothing can be said with certainty except that many were one syllable and therefore are not likely to be two morphemes, even in Brenda's system. The conclusion, of course, is simply that Dale is wrong.

The selected count of (162) may, perhaps, give an indication of how Dale's conclusion could have been reached. For (162) I selected all of the stretches of utterances that included horizontal constructions such as in (12) above, the *wash clothes* example. If some one-word utterances were in close proximity, they were counted, otherwise they were not. With this kind of selection, I got the figures for (162). Even with this kind of selection, horizontal construction accounts for only 47.4 percent of the total.

TABLE 19. Distribution of Utterances in BRENDA III

		Number	*Percentage*
(161)	One-word	186	53.4
	Two-word	77	22.1
	Unintelligible but can be transcribed	77	22.1
	Not transcribable	8	2.4
	Total	348	100.0
(162)	(Selected 185 out of 500 "feet" of tape)		
	One-word	80	45.7
	Two-word	83	47.4
	Unintelligible but can be transcribed	7	4.0
	Not transcribable	5	2.9
	Total	175	100.0

Of course, doing a little arithmetic with the mean of 1.46 would indicate that "two-word utterances" could not possibly be the "most common" type of language. That my figures are generally representative of this stage is borne out by Brown (1973, p. 138) who says that "in the 713 utterances of Adam I there are 202 which consist of two or more words." Presumably he is referring to tokens. The percentage that this gives is 28.3 percent compared to BRENDA III's 22.1 percent. Brown further reports that "from a corpus of 713 utterances Bowerman obtained 110 distinct combinations (types)." This gives a percentage of 15.4 percent. This can be compared to BRENDA III's 9.4 percent (types).

VII.7.2   Vertical Construction in BRENDA III

By now it should be clear that the horizontal constructions of BRENDA III compare favorably with those presented by other investigators for children at this stage of development. In my discussion of vertical construction in BRENDA II, I said that Brenda had arrived at the threshold of horizontal construction and that this was by a process of active practice in construction. What is spectacular is that these processes of vertical construction do not lead into horizontal construction as into a dead end. When horizontal construction relieves vertical construction of the burden of two-word construction, the constructional possibilities are simply multiplied. The list of horizontal constructions of BRENDA III in Table 18 has been presented much as constructions of this kind have appeared in the published data on this period. What startled me was to place these horizontal constructions back into the context of the tape from which they were taken and discover the vertical constructions in which they function. Look at these:

<pre>
(13)   (161)57   Brenda
             58   see that

             89   my turn
             90   do it
</pre>

Table 20 gives a full list of the vertical construction of BRENDA III (161–162). For some time, investigators have lamented the fact that we have only performance data to look at. It has been said that what we need is some kind of evidence for the more complex structures that we feel the child must understand at this time, that the horizontal constructions imply knowledge of more elaborate constructional ability. For this child, Brenda, there is a great deal of evidence. Look at E3 and E8. The vertical construction in both cases produces subject-verb-object, which is adult Standard English word order. Horizontal constructions imply that it is known. In vertical constructions it actually shows up in speech. In *my turn. do it* we even have a construction corresponding to the structurally complex adult form *It's my turn to do it.*

Notice that there are several varieties of vertical construction in Table 20. In fact, just the same varieties are present here as in the earlier period (BRENDA II). Numbers E3, E5, E6, E8, E22, and E33 correspond to type A in which the elements in construction are not repeated, and closely follow each other without the intervention of another speaker. Notice that now a vertical construction may have three elements and that any of those elements may be a horizontal construction. That is, when the single utterance limit went up from one morpheme to two morphemes, the limit on vertical constructions went from two to three elements. This suggests that later further expansion might take place.

The final point about this type A construction is that, as earlier, this type of vertical construction is the rarest. This is interesting in that these show the highest degree of complexity in terms of adult syntax. In the same way that *finger.touch* represented the highest point in the development of one-word vertical construction, *Ron.make.tapecorder* or *my turn.do it* may represent the highest point in the development of two-word horizontal component vertical construction.

The second type of vertical construction, type B, allows repetition of any of the elements. In example E7, *use it* is repeated. E30 is also of this type. Again, there is a feeling of difficulty in performance that is surmounted by the technique of repetition.

Types C and D have another speaker intervening in discourse with Brenda. Notice in E7 that the speaker asked Brenda a question that prompted her response.

It is important to mention again that these examples were all taken from a single hour of tape. In this case, we are not looking at a developmental history. All of these types are present during the same hour, and I have no general indication of development for

TABLE 20. Vertical Constructions in BRENDA III

E1	Ron (R) O.K. Ron talk		E10	dat one cat (2x) dis cat dis
E2	turning (3x) turning around		E11	rottened. rotten food (3x) dog some doggie some doggie
E3	Brenda see that			
E4	tape corder (2x) [bɪkut] in there. k?		E12	more gone more more coming out
E5	tape corder in there		E13	there Daddy
E6	my turn do it		E14	picture mark this this this way
E7	tape corder. (R) Yeah. use it (2x) (R) Use it for what? talk corder talk Brenda talk		E15	picture mark this way (2x)
			E16	[æʔ] hiding Halet hiding Halet (R) Who's hiding Charlotte?
E8	Ron make tape corder corder tape		E17	hiding Brenda (2x) (R) Where? Brenda hiding (2x)
E9	sleeping (5x) (R) Who's sleeping? Cat sleeping in the book. cat sleeping		E18	banana leaf (2x) pick it (6x)

TABLE 20—*Continued*

E19	Brenda	E28	writing (2x)
	This way		read dat
	picture mark		
	dis is way	E29	cut it down (2x)
	this way (2x)		strong
			read dat (2x)
E20	bend it		
	bend	E30	monster (4x)
	bend it (2x)		swim
			water
E21	this way		
	hold it (3x)	E31	scared (2x)
	holding (2x)		monster eat
			scared (4x)
E22	rabbit		
	put it on	E32	horn off (4x)
			bring it home (2x)
E23	dere		bring home
	found it		bring it home
			bring
E24	cookie		
	ee	E33	scary monster
	monster go		read dat
E25	soup (4x)	E34	take home
	(R) What? What are		taked it home
	you talking about?		home
	drink soup		
		E35	horn off
E26	wash clothing		bring it home (8x)
	wash (3x)		
	wash clothes (2x)	E36	like that
			like that song
E27	tree down		
	tree		

this period. By now, however, the continuity with the earlier period should be clear. Vertical construction is a phenomenon that develops during the prehorizontal construction period and remains active at least well into this period.

One further point of continuity that will be taken up again in VIII.3.1 on the internal structure of these constructions is that many of these vertical constructions seem to be topic-comment structures. For instance, *writing.writing.read dat* was said while I was reading a story to Brenda that included a section where the boy in the story was learning to write. The meaning of Brenda's construction was 'read the part about writing', which was further evidenced by her leafing through the pages until she found that picture. These topic-comment constructions are, by far, the most plentiful of the vertical constructions in this sample. In retrospect, this type of construction can be seen to have developed in the interaction Brenda has had with other speakers. It is very tempting to think that vertical construction, which is first learned in discourse, ultimately remains at the foundation of the structure of discourse. I have tried to show that for this earliest period of horizontal construction there was a preceding period of vertical construction as preparation. Further, during the first period of horizontal construction, vertical construction remained active in producing the prototypes of longer horizontal constructions of later periods. This suggests, in fact, that discourse structure is at the heart of sentence structure from the beginning of its development.

CHAPTER VIII

The Structure of Constructions

VIII.1 How Can We Know Structure?

The question of just what it is we are describing when we describe a "child's language" has been brought up before. There is no part of the discussion where this problem is more central than here in the discussion of the internal structure of constructions. In the chapter before this, it was fairly easy to talk about the external forms of construction. To begin with, in the early tapes an utterance could be defined as being bounded by silence. Later, but still in the early periods (BRENDA I and II), utterances could be defined by stress and falling intonation contour coupled with boundaries of silence. In these early periods, "word" could be taken as equivalent to "utterance" without fear of serious misrepresentation.

The onset of horizontal construction produced a redefinition of utterance. That is, utterance was still defined as being bounded by silence and receiving primary stress and terminal contour, but it was no longer equivalent to "word." The definition of "word" was something like "former utterances." Words could be separated within horizontal constructions on the basis of their presence as single utterances in the preceding period. Vertical constructions could be defined on the basis of these other definitions, first as sequences of words and then as sequences of horizontal constructions.

The assumptions that have to be made are relatively few and, perhaps, innocent of misrepresentation. One assumes that silence does define utterance boundaries for the child. One further assumes that primary stress and terminal intonation contour have come to have the same meaning in the child's system as in the adult system.

VIII.1.1   Internal Structure

The problem of inferring the internal structure of utterances is not restricted to child language studies. Without going into the difficulties of distributional analysis of adult speech, it should be mentioned that the approach of Braine (1963, 1971) appears to be modeled after such studies of adult speech as that of Fries (1952), in which an attempt is made to infer the internal structure of the utterances without reference to a speaker's intuitions about that structure. Of course, by now it is abundantly clear that Braine's attempt failed. It was only successful to the extent that he had removed from analysis conflicting forms. One of the major problems is, as Bloom (1970, p. 29) points out, that "there are no inflectional criteria for identifying major categories." She argues that in order to get "evidence for constructing grammars for children's language it appears to be necessary to depend on the intuitions of a native speaker of the mature language for interpreting the semantic intention of what the child says" (p. 9). Bloom's major assumption is that it is "possible to reach the semantics of children's sentences by considering nonlinguistic information from context and behavior in relation to linguistic performance" (p. 10). In order to break into the closed circle of the child's system, Bloom has found it necessary to refer to her own linguistic system. Specifically, she has done this by taking nouns to represent a "given" category. She says (p. 30), "The feature [+N] was assigned to all lexical items that have noun status in the adult model. All lexical items, including nouns, were charted according to their occurrence in environments with nouns."

There is precedent for this procedure. For example, Brown and Bellugi-Klima (1964, 1971, p. 308) describe their method as follows:

> For many purposes we require a 'distributional analysis' of the speech of the child. To this end the child's utterances in a given transcription were cross classified and relisted under such headings as: 'A noun'; 'Noun-Verb'; 'Verbs in the past'; 'Utterances containing the pronoun

it'; etc. The categorized utterances expose the syntactic regularities of the child's speech.

In this case there was no attempt to restrict the number of "givens." All words were assumed to be susceptible to categorization within the adult system.

The extreme to which this type of categorization has been pushed can be seen best by referring to several of McNeill's publications. McNeill's 1970 book raises the question of how a child could have learned the basic grammatical categories. That the child has learned such things is simply asserted on the basis of his earlier publication—McNeill 1966. It is true that in McNeill 1966 he raises the question of what the status of such categories as noun and verb for the child might be. But to resolve the difficulty, McNeill refers to the source quoted above, Brown and Bellugi-Klima, where we have seen that these categories were simply asserted in the process of transcription. While giving the appearance of dealing with the problem of "givens," McNeill pushed the resolution back onto earlier "word," which did not come to grips with the problem either.

VIII.1.2   Grammatical Categories in Child Language

Clearly, if grammatical categories are simply asserted for child language and then taken as being the primary data that a theory of language must explain, the circularity must be condemned. On the other hand, as a means of breaking into the child's system, a cautious use of "givens" that are based on adult intuitions can be justified.

In the first place, it is clear that the child's utterances do communicate. I think it can be assumed that for communication to take place between the child's system and the adult's system there must be some nontrivial overlap. Brown (1973, p. 106) has recommended taking the "parental view." This recommendation amounts to making Bloom's assumption that if context is carefully considered one can understand some things about the child's system. That this is, in fact, the parental view is demonstrated in the following interaction between Brenda and her mother.

(1) (131)   (B is playing in the sandbox outside the house and there are quite a few flies around)

217   fai
218   fwə

(M) Yeah, a lot of flies. Go fishing
with these flies. Catch your flies.

Whatever these two utterances were in Brenda's system the mother
has taken them to be nouns (*fly.fly*) and relevant in the context
as saying something about the abundance of flies. Further, she has
immediately demonstrated the adult plural inflection for this
category and given three sentence frames into which it can be put.
In other words the "parental view" is to assume that Brenda has
said a noun and act on that assumption.

It is still possible that Brenda's system is different from the
adult's. But whatever else these utterances are in her system, they
overlap with nouns in the adult system. The child's communication
is dependent on this overlap, and it is reasonable to assume that she
will communicate to the extent that she accepts and, in turn,
understands the parental view. The development of the child's
words seems to indicate that this is what happens. By the time she
begins horizontal construction, the majority of the child's words
may be classed as if they were adult words (to the extent that adult
words can be successfully classed!) and the resulting word orders
also fit the adult semantic system. Brown (1973, p. 145) refers to
Bloom (1970) when he says,

> the child's speech contains a certain kind of evidence that the relations
> are in his mind, and not just in the mind of the adult interpreter;
> the evidence of word order. The child acquiring English in a huge
> majority of cases orders his words as they should be ordered if the
> semantic relations suggested by context to adults are what he intends.

Of course this matching is somewhat guaranteed by the
fact that the adult refers to the semantic context to infer word
classes. For example, one of the difficult utterances that will be
mentioned later is *picture mark*. What is in question is the correct
category of *mark*. (In another context even the category of *picture*
would be open to question.) Is Brenda saying that the picture
will get marked or that the picture will get a mark? The inferred
semantic structure depends on the word class, and the word class
depends on the semantic structure. If this had been, for instance,
black mark the first word would be more easily classed as adjective

and the second as noun. On the other hand, something like *pen mark* would be more easily taken as a noun–verb construction.

What is the parental view in this case?

(2) (161)   (B is holding some photographs carefully with both hands cupped under them)

  208   picture mark
  209   this
  210   this
  211   this way
                 (M) x x x make marks. Gotta hold it that way.

It is clear that the parental view is that *mark* is a noun. This raises the question of how to decide when the parental view is correct. A simple reference to the immediate context in this case is not sufficient. I was present and took *mark* as a verb. Although this is a descriptive statement of what I did think, the reason I took *mark* as a verb is that I thought she was saying she was going to mark the picture (that is, by not holding it correctly). In this particular case, however, the mother has apparently drilled Brenda on the treatment of pictures and has said something of this sort to her before. Just what she has said on other occasions cannot be determined, but in the conflict between her intuition of Brenda's word class and mine in this case I would have to decide in favor of the mother's.

In most cases, intuitions of word class can be made somewhat more reliably than this by simple reference to the context, as in this case it is difficult to consider *picture* a verb because of the context. I have presented a particularly difficult example so that the tentative nature of the use of "givens" (as in the case of *mark*) will be apparent. I can conclude this discussion by saying that my approach has followed Bloom's. I feel that this technique of using "givens" is justified as long as one realizes that what is described is the communicative overlap between the two systems, not the child's own system, which remains inaccessible. In this context, when I say that the child's system is developing I am referring to an increase in the overlap between the child's system and the adult system. This can be inferred from the increased ease with which the adult and the child can understand each other.

VIII.2   Structure of Horizontal Constructions

In this discussion, I am going to look at the horizontal constructions of BRENDA III (161–162), age 1;10.17. Remember that this is one hour of tape that was first taken only with the intention of providing a follow-up of BRENDA I and BRENDA II. Because of the relatively small amount of basic data that I have to work with, I have applied no criterion of "productivity" such as that applied by Bloom (1972, p. 29). In general her approach of including only structures that occurred more than once would not work in such a narrow format as this. What is surprising, however, is the extent of agreement between the forms that have appeared in (161–162) and the forms reported by other investigators for children at the same period in their development (as summarized in Brown 1973, p. 66).

Table 18 (VII.7.1) listed all of the horizontal constructions of (161–162)—types not tokens. As a first approach, I listed them in groups on the basis of adult word classes. Within each group, all of the forms fit into roughly the same patterns. I should also mention that in addition to these ten groups there are the isolated one-word utterances that might be said to form four other groups. On this tape, the one-word utterances may be classified as nouns (e.g., *Ron, mirror, T.V., snowman*), verbs in a progressive form (e.g., *turning, moving, singing*), adjectives (e.g., *ugly, blue, green*), and negatives (e.g., *no, don't*).

The ten groups of Table 18 can be described as follows:

(3) *Group 1*: noun—verb. Notice that *more* in *more coming out* has been grouped as a noun here. Braine (1963, 1971) has *more* as a pivot. Schlesinger, as reported in Brown (1973, p. 114), includes *more* as an object (and presumably, therefore a noun). I have considered it to be a noun here by analogy with *Peach Boy coming out*.

$$\textit{Group 2}: \text{verb} - \left|\begin{array}{c} \text{noun} \\ \textit{it} \end{array}\right|.$$ I have mentioned before (VII.7.1; also see VIII.4) that I think *it* here functions as an inflectional particle indicating transitivization of the verb. This is on the basis of the more or less complete lack of independence from the verb. However, by comparison with the other forms in this group, *it* appears in the same position as the nouns and the pronouns *dat, that*, and *this*, for example, *read dat* and *read it*. This would indicate,

perhaps, some rudimentary status as a pronoun for *it*. For these pronouns and *it*, I am making no distinction between noun and pronoun.

Group 3: noun—noun. The difficulty of *picture mark* has been discussed above. *Key lock* is equally vague. *Key* is less doubtful than *lock*. The context is not helpful in this case. Brenda may either be speaking of putting the key in the lock or locking the door with the key.

Group 4: complex verbs. These are the separable verbs. Notice the number of cases in which *it* appears optionally between the two parts of the verb, for example, *bring home* and *bring it home*. Notice also *fill it up* and *fill up it* in which *it* shows some independence. Finally, *tree down* and *horn off* are clearly exceptional, but I have grouped them here because of *cut it down*. This grouping will be discussed in VIII.4 below.

Group 5: noun—noun phrase (locative). The relationships between groups 5 and 6 will be taken up later (VIII.4). Here, I am tentatively considering *here* and *dere* to be NP's because they occupy the same position as the rudimentary NP *on it*.

Group 6: preposition—pronoun (locative).

Group 7: modifier—noun. Even for adult speech it is not clear to what class *banana* in *banana leaf* belongs. Brenda has used both words separately since BRENDA II as nouns. In this case, however, the first word stands in the relation of modifier to the second.

Group 8: pronoun (demonstrative)—noun. Only two of the four in this group literally fit this description: *dis cat* and *this way* (the orthographic contrast between *d* and *th* represents Brenda's variation between [d] and [ð]). *Dat one cat* appears to have expanded the demonstrative pronoun into a full NP. *This is way* was one instance in which the copula was inserted.

Group 9: noun—pronoun (quantifying). The reasons I have considered *some* to be a quantifier rather than a noun (see *more* above) are to keep these separate from group 2 (noun—noun) and because this *some* has occurred regularly since BRENDA II with a quite rigid meaning of a quantity of something that Brenda gives to someone else.

Group 10: no restrictions. This includes idiomatic phrases such as *thank you*, and Brenda's longest single utterance, from (151) *Santa Claus says Ho, Ho, Ho, Merry Christmas*.

VIII.2.1   A Richer Interpretation

After the classification of utterances given in (3) above, the question remains of what it is worth. Perhaps it is interesting to see that a child of this age has the variety of constructions I have shown. However, without some demonstration that these different structures have a meaning that is different from that of the two words taken separately, not much has been said. Bloom (1970, p. 7) has pointed out that it is "necessary for grammars of child language to do more than just describe the surface constituents of sentences that can occur." Brown (1973), in reviewing child language studies reported during the last decade, notices that the general movement has been from distributional studies in the beginning to what he calls the "rich interpretation" exhibited in more current work. In the discussion that follows, I am going to skip over the intermediate approach that would discuss the forms grouped above in terms of their "grammatical" structure. By this I mean that I am not going to be particularly concerned with the apparent fact that the constructions in group 1 resemble adult sentences while those of groups 6 and 7 resemble adult NP's. What I am going to do now is take up Brown's prediction that studies of child language will confirm that at this stage of horizontal construction the child has control of three operations and a small set (around eight) of semantic relations.

VIII.2.2   The Three Operations

Brown (1973, p. 189–198) defines three operations of reference and eight semantic relations that were found expressed in the language of stage I (MLU 1;0–2;0) children. The three operations he defines are nomination, recurrence, and nonexistence.

Nomination is expressed when the referent of an utterance is "made manifest by some action calling attention to it for the members of the communicating group, usually a dyad"'(p. 189). This can work from either direction. That is, the adult may point to something and ask "What's that?" The child's answer expresses nomination. From the other side of the dyad, the child's utterances, such as *this x* or *here x*, when accompanied by pointing indicate nomination.

Brown refers to recurrence as it is demonstrated in Bloom's data by instances of *more* plus a noun or verb.

The construction either comments on (declarative) or requests (imperative) 'recurrence' of a thing, person, or process. Recurrence itself means different things in different cases. It may mean the reappearance of the same referent already seen; it may mean the appearance of a new instance of a referent class of which one instance has already been seen, and it may mean an additional quantity (or 'helping') of some mass of which a first quantity has already been seen. (p. 190)

Nonexistence expresses the opposite of recurrence.

In very many cases, as terms like *all gone* and *no more* would suggest, the present nonexistent was quite recently existent in the reference context. (p. 192)

Brown suggests that "disappearance" might be more accurate than "nonexistence" in these cases. He points out, however, that "what is essential is an expectation of existence which the nonexistence sentence disappoints." (p. 192)

The presence of two of Brown's three operations, nomination and nonexistence, can be easily confirmed from BRENDA III. Recurrence is somewhat more difficult to establish.

Dat one cat and *dis cat* exactly fit Brown's description of nomination. It is interesting that many of the single-word utterances (that is, utterances that are in neither horizontal nor vertical construction) also are clear cases of nomination. For example, Brenda was looking into the cassette tape recorder, which has a clear plastic door. At first she was watching the tape turn but then suddenly said, *mirror!* Her loud voice indicated to me her surprise at the discovery of the reflecting properties of the plastic. Nomination of this sort is frequent and the easiest of these operations to establish. Some of the utterances of group 7 were also of this type. For example, *icy juicy* was said as Brenda looked into a glass of juice with ice that her mother had just given her.

Recurrence may be expressed by *more* in *more coming out*.

The use of *hiding* indicates nonexistence for Brenda. It is equivalent to *allgone* as discussed by Brown (1973). In the examples of *hiding* in Table 18, Brenda was looking at photographs in which many members of her extended family were present. It was while looking at just those photographs in which she didn't appear that she said, *hiding Brenda. Hiding Halet* was then said of Charlotte for one photograph in which Charlotte did not appear. Brenda is commenting on the absence of the person expected.

VIII.2.3   The Semantic Relations

Brown gives eight relations as the basic core of semantic relations (p. 193–198). They are

(4) (1) agent and action
      (2) action and object
      (3) agent and object
      (4) action and locative
      (5) entity and locative
      (6) possessor and possession
      (7) entity and attribute
      (8) demonstrative and entity

Before discussing these eight semantic relations, there is one concept that I feel needs specific mention. That is the concept of "agent." In general, agents are taken to have the feature of [+ animate] (e.g., Fillmore, 1968). This feature has been applied by reference to the investigator's own feelings about what is animate and what is inanimate. What I want to point out is that it is difficult to say what the animate/inanimate distinction might mean for a child. Piaget (1969, p. 229) has said that "the child's thought begins with a lack of differentiation between living and inert bodies." In another place he says that in the first stage (age 4 to 6;7) "all things are conscious—the child in this stage certainly never says that everything is conscious. He simply says that any object may be the seat of consciousness at a given moment, that is to say when the object displays a particular measure of activity or is the seat of some action" (p. 174).

It is probably true, then, that Brenda at 1;10.17 does not make any distinction between animate and inanimate or conscious and nonconscious. For this reason, it is likely that for her "agent" and "object" are probably not distinguished on the basis of the feature [animate]. (Several years later, age 3;7, Brenda was still inquiring about a five-month-old infant if she was real and if she was alive.) I am following Brown's (and Chafe 1970) usage in not requiring this distinction for agents.

I should also point out that the three operations are not distinct from the eight semantic relations as a separate set of utterances. That is, an utterance that expresses one of the semantic relations may also express one of the operations. For example, the two utterances *dat one cat* and *dis cat* both express nomination (an operation) as well as demonstrative and entity (a semantic relation).

The groups of Table 18 can be matched up with Brown's eight semantic relations as follows:

(5) (1) agent and action: Group 1. If we remember that agent is not strictly animate, the inclusion of *more* and *corder* as agents is not particularly incongruent.

(2) action and object: Group 2. Some of these are less clearly objects than others. I have included *it* as an object. Considering *see*, *hiding*, and *have* as actions in relation to objects is also somewhat strained.

(3) agent and object: Group 3. *Picture mark* is certainly not expressing this relation. That is, it is very difficult to imagine that Brenda is saying the picture has instigated some action that has resulted or will result in the mark. *Key lock* may or may not be in this relation. It could only be expressing this relation if she meant that the key had done something to the lock, which seems rather farfetched. On the whole I feel that I have no examples of this relation. Brown (1973) suggests that children vary on the use of this construction.

(4) action and locative: Group 4. Some of the constructions in this group may be of this type. For example, *bring home* and *bring it home* through the structure of a separable verb seem to indicate both the action and movement toward a location. There are others, such as *leave it on* and *put it on*, for which locative does not seem to be too strong a classification. However, such complex verbs as *fill up* and *cut it down* are more indicative, for me, of the finished state of the main verb than location. For me, to fill up means to fill until it cannot be filled any further, not fill toward the top. I can only guess what they might mean for Brenda. The isomorphy of *up* in *fill up* with *up* in such adult utterances as *come up* and *climb up* may mean that for Brenda they are in some way locative.

One further note on these complex verbs. If the two parts of the separable verb indicate an action and locative relationship, there is still room in this construction for an optional *it* that may indicate object as well. The variation between noun and *it* that has been mentioned before will be discussed in more detail below.

(5) entity and locative: Groups 5 and 6. The examples of group 5 have a clear entity stated, that is, *who*, *Brenda*, and *water*. In these, the locative is expressed by *dere*, *here* and the noun phrase *on it*. Group 6 constructions do not have any entity expressed but are full noun phrases. As I will try to show later, at least in one case this entity is expressed in vertical construction, that is, *tape corder. in there*. The relationship between these two groups will be discussed below as having to do with the two-constituent limit on horizontal construction.

(6) possessor and possession: Group 3. In this case *key lock* can be definitely excluded as expressing this relation. *Picture mark* is probably of this type. That is to say, it is not unreasonable to think that this construction means that the picture will have a mark (if not treated properly). It is the only example in (161–162) that may be of this relation.

(7) entity and attribute: Group 7. To the extent that items in this group are genuine constructions, they all may be considered to express this relation. I have doubts about the constructional status of some of these. *Banana leaf* and *paper napkin* may be single words. Only two of group 7, *scary monster* and *icy juicy*, are very probably constructions of this type.

(8) demonstrative and entity: Group 8. In one case the demonstrative has been expanded to a full noun phrase—*dat one*. In the other case, the copula has been inserted between the two elements of the relation.

This covers the eight basic relations that Brown has suggested. He does not claim that these are the only eight relations nor that all of these invariably occur. In addition to this list of eight are several others that have at least marginal status. I have evidence for least two of these.

(9) indirect object dative: Group 9. There is only one example of this structure on this tape (161–162). Several days earlier 151–152), Brenda used this construction extensively but always with a regular meaning. In all of the other cases, the construction was proper noun—*some*. The meaning was 'I am giving some of this to X'. As I will point out below the object in this construction occurs in vertical construction, for example, *rotten. food. dog some*.

(10) instrumental: Group 3. One analysis of *key lock* would have *key* as an instrument and *lock* as an action. This is the

only case, and, since I have mentioned this example in several other relations, it should be clear that its status is, at best, quite tentative.

Finally, there are the forms of group 10 that are apparently unrestricted and include idiomatic phrases and memorized performances such as the Santa Claus quote mentioned above (VIII.2). It should be noted, however, that this unrestricted miscellany does not include any utterances simply because they are problematic for the analysis above. That is, I have not used this miscellany as a means of getting rid of difficult cases.

VIII.2.4   Summary

To conclude this review of Brown's three operations and eight semantic relations, I can say that there is a fair correspondence between his predictions and my data. In some of the cases the relationships have been quite clear, but in others it has been difficult to make decisions about the correct classification of an utterance. The groups of Table 18 were originally grouped on the basis of the similarity of the internal structuring of the order of word classes. I have shown that, in general, these internal structures express distinct semantic relations. I say "in general" because several of these groups do not seem to have any one semantic structure associated with them. For example, group 3 (noun—noun) structures are difficult to be certain about in the first place, and do not, as a group, express a single relation. At the other extreme, two groups, 5 and 6, seem to be collapsible in the expression of one relation—entity and locative.

The result is that there is not always a one-to-one correspondence between the expressive means and the expressed relation. It is also interesting that the cases that are easiest to classify happen to have word orders that correspond to adult surface orders. The noun-verb constructions are easy to understand as agent and object relations. On the other hand, noun-noun constructions are not responsive to a neat analysis. This should signal to us again that we are studying the overlap between the child's system and the adult's system. On the one hand, there is evidence that the child is using some of the same expressive means as the adult. The evidence for this is that so many of the child's utterances fit fairly easily into the adult classifications. On the other hand, the lack of total fit indicates both that the child's system is not isomorphic with the adult's and that our intuitions about the adult's system may not be correct either.

To recapitulate, then, I have found quite clear evidence for Brown's three operations—nomination, recurrence, and nonexistence. For the basic semantic relations I have found the following:

(6)   (1) agent and action: strong evidence.
      (2) action and object: strong evidence.
      (3) agent and object: probably not present.
      (4) action and locative: moderate evidence.
      (5) entity and locative: good evidence.
      (6) possessor and possession: probably present, but the evidence is one weak case.
      (7) entity and attribute: moderate evidence.
      (8) demonstrative and entity: moderate evidence.
      (9) indirect object dative: one good example.
     (10) instrumental: only one doubtful example.
     (11) unrestricted: several examples.

This part of my analysis is based on a limited sample of one hour with around 600 total utterances, which may be compared with data summarized in Brown (1973, p. 65–74). Brown used 713 utterances each for the "grammars" written for Adam, Eve, and Sarah. Bowerman also used 713 utterances as her data base for a "grammar." Braine used 293 utterances and Miller and Ervin used 450. Bloom's "grammars" are based on totals as follows: Eric I, 19; Eric II, 87; Gia I, 141; Kathryn I, 397; Gia II, 141; and Eric III, 243.

I feel that Brown's predictions are strongly confirmed. That is, most of the relations he claims are present. The ones that are not present may have been excluded by the narrow limits of the sample. On the other hand, the evidence for relations other than those mentioned by Brown is weak. Generally speaking, Brown's operations and relations appear to be an appropriate categorization of the horizontal constructions in my data. In a confirmation of this sort, however, I want to recall that we are looking at the overlap of two linguistic systems, Brenda's and mine. What I am confirming is not necessarily that Brenda's system fits this characterization but that my understanding of Brenda's system fits with the understanding other investigators have had of the systems they have studied. I believe that this is certainly indicative of some characteristics of the child's own system but not that this description is the child's system.

VIII.3   Structure of Vertical Constructions

Bloom (1972, p. 25) makes the following mention of what I call vertical construction: "It is of considerable interest that just before the emergence of syntax in their speech, Gia, Eric, Allison, and Leopold's Hildegard were able to produce related one-word utterances in succession, but without underlying grammatical relationship between the forms." In Chapter 7, I have claimed that there is a relationship between the forms that make up vertical constructions, and that this relationship can be seen to be grammatical. In his discussion of longer sentences, Brown (1973, p. 187) concludes that more complex sentences (e.g. *Adam hit ball*) can be seen as combinations of the elements *Adam hit* and *hit ball*. He further claims that the child has to learn to do this. The claim I make is that vertical construction is an important process by which he learns to do this. In the discussion that follows, I intend to show how the separate structures of horizontal construction combine to produce structures of greater length and complexity.

Table 20 (VII.7.2) listed all of the vertical constructions of (161–162). Again as an approach, we can list forms on the basis of word classes and Brown's semantic relations. For horizontal constructions, I found ten types of word class structures:

(7)   (1) noun—verb
    (2) verb— $\left| \begin{matrix} \text{noun} \\ it \end{matrix} \right|$
    (3) noun—noun
    (4) complex verbs
    (5) noun—noun phrase (locative)
    (6) preposition—pronoun (locative)
    (7) modifier—noun
    (8) pronoun (demonstrative)—noun
    (9) noun—pronoun (quantifying)
  (10) unrestricted

In addition to the ten types of horizontal constructions above, there were four single word types: noun, verb, adjective, and negative.

The following types of vertical construction can be found in Table 20.

(8)	(1)	E3	noun	agent
			verb—noun	action and object
	(2)	E8	noun	agent
			verb	action
			modifier—noun	object
	(3)	E6	modifier—noun	entity and attribute
			verb—noun	action and object
	(4)	E21	pronoun (demonstra-	demonstrative and
			tive)—noun	entity
			verb—noun	action and object
			verb	?
	(5)	E5	noun	object
			preposition—	entity and locative
			pronoun (locative)	
	(6)	E7	noun	object
			verb—noun	action and object
			verb	action
			noun—verb	agent and action
			noun—verb	agent and action
	(7)	E18	modifier—noun	entity and attribute
			verb—noun	action and object
	(8)	E22	noun	object
			complex verb	action and locative
	(9)	E28	verb	object
			verb—noun	action and object

This is only a partial list of the vertical constructions of Table 20, but it will serve to illustrate several problems. First, it should be noticed that with the exception of (6) the same type of horizontal construction does not appear more than once in any vertical construction. Type (6) is a very weak case of vertical construction. It appears to be more a pattern drill of some kind than a construction. On the other hand, I should point out that it is just because two horizontal constructions or the same type appear in sequence that this does not seem to be much of a construction. My inclination is to believe that the prohibition of two horizontal constructions of the same type within a single vertical construction is a characteristic of the child's system, but I have included (7) in the list of vertical constructions to keep the data honest even if it makes it difficult to generalize the dissimilar element restriction. In this I am acknowledging the importance of Labov's call to remain true to the data in spite of theoretical difficulties (Labov 1970; 1971).

In the first example, it seems clear from the context of the action and object construction with which it forms a vertical construction that the single noun *Brenda* is an agent (*Brenda. see that*). The second example, *Ron. make. tape corder*, gives a structure of agent and action and object.

Examples (3) and (7) give instances of a horizontal construction that is entity and attribute functioning in a higher semantic relation. In (3) *my turn. do it*, it is not clear what the relation of *my turn* to *do it* is except that it is *not* object. It may be agent. In (7), *banana leaf.* (2x) *pick it* (6x), the entity and attribute relation functions as object in the whole.

This compounding of levels only seems to happen for one other of the basic semantic relations. Above, I somewhat tentatively grouped *in there* and *on dere* with entity and locative. In (5) *in there* occurs in construction with *tape corder*. It seems clear that when there is an "entity" expressed in vertical construction it is not expressed in the horizontal locative construction. Only when the "entity" is within the same horizontal construction as in *Brenda here*, is it really an entity and locative construction. Otherwise, it is simply a locative noun phrase.

It is peculiar that the two pairs of relations, entity and attribute and entity and locative, may function as single elements in a higher level semantic relation (e.g., entity and attribute becomes object in an object-action-object construction in *banana leaf. pick it*). It is because I want to suggest this hierarchical structure that I have used "noun phrase."

VIII.3.1 Topic-Comment Constructions

There are two general types of vertical constructions in Table 20. The first type has adult English word order, for example, E3, *Brenda. see that*, E8, *Ron. make. tape corder*, and E6, *my turn. do it*. For these, there seems to be a general principle of nonredundancy operating. That is, a relation does not occur twice in the same construction.

The second type of vertical construction has just this prohibited redundancy. Notice that in some cases in Table 20 there is one case relation—object—that occurs twice, for example, E28, *writing.* (2x) *read dat.* E7, E11, E22, E29, E33, and others are also examples of this. Bloom (1972, p. 24) has said about constructions of this type that "a structural description of these utterances in terms of Topic and Comment as the basic grammatical relation of (the) surface structure of the constituents (Chomsky, 1965, p. 221) would be appropriate." Bloom says further (p. 25) that "at this stage, when children produce utterances with the surface features of Topic and Comment, they do not use the syntax of the adult model, and there is no evidence from their linguistic performance that they 'know' the syntax in the sense of being able to use it." To be fair, I should make clear that Bloom was referring to an earlier stage of development (corresponding to BRENDA II).

The point I wish to make is that many of the vertical constructions of this period can be described as Topic-Comment constructions. They can be more explicitly described as constructions of the form: Object/action (*writing/read*) plus object (*dat*) in which the object (*writing*, i.e., 'the part about writing') occurs twice in the construction.

The abundance of these forms in this hour of tape and their productivity lead me to question Bloom's assertion that "there is is no evidence from their linguistic performance that they 'know' the syntax." Gruber (1967, 1971, p. 343) makes a fairly strong case for Topic-Comment structures but then, unfortunately, assumes that because they are not present in the parents' speech they must represent some innate ability of the child. First, I should point out that Topic-Comment constructions are present in Brenda's parents' speech. But even in the cases where these constructions are not present in the adult speech, I suggest that they are learned by the child not in imitation of the adult but rather in interactions with adults.

VIII.4   Constraint on Length

Brown and Bellugi-Klima (1964, 1971, p. 310) observed that their children "were operating under some constraint of length or span." They further suggest that "the constraint is a limitation on the length of utterance the children are able to program or plan." Bloom (1970) observed that "the affirmative sentence was reduced with the operation of negation" (p. 169). She further points out: "the number of syntactic operations or the complexity of grammatical relationships within a sentence appears to increase the cognitive weight of the sentence for the child, and his reduced utterance reflects the inability to carry the full sentence load in performance." More recently, Brown (1973, p. 184) has said: "Sentence complexity limits in Stage I may be stated in terms of the number of elementary relations that may be programmed into a single sentence."

This overall constraint on the length of an utterance is observable in the data I have offered. An examination of this phenomenon shows some interesting results. The explanation for this constraint that comes to mind is that a young child simply does not have any more complex underlying structure than that expressed, and the length of the surface forms must wait on this cognitive development. The vertical constructions, however, indicate that in some cases, at least, Brenda does have in mind a larger structure than that which can be said in one utterance. That is, there may be a natural limitation on the length of utterances. This limitation is overcome with development so that constructions that were only possible vertically—that is, with pauses, later become possible horizontally.

If there is a natural limitation on length, then there should be cases where under certain conditions that limit can be lifted as is the case in phonology where if there is an immediate model of the word, the pronunciation can be somewhat advanced over that normally found for that stage. Or in some cases, we should see evidence of improvement with practice over several repetitions. As we will now see, in construction there are cases of several phenomena that do indicate a natural limitation.

Two of the several cases of longer than two-word horizontal constructions appear to be simply innovative, that is, *Brenda read now* and *now read it*. Also *more coming out* and *Peach Boy coming out* have been discussed above as not being real violations if a constituent may include such complex proper nouns as *Peach Boy*.

There are several cases where Brenda builds up a longer form over several repetitions. The last time the *this way* sequence appears it is *this* [ɪ] *way*. There is apparently an attempt to insert a copula between the two elements. This sequence, however, is apparently a rehearsed sequence.

A clearer case yet is that of *like that* followed by *like that song.* In this case, Brenda does manage to include a full noun phrase in an action and object structure. This sequence is partly modeled by my question several minutes earlier, *You like that? You like that story, Brenda?*

The most noticeable examples of the two-word, or constituent, limit have to do with the use of *it.* There are many cases in which a complex verb occurs first without *it* and then with *it* between the two elements, for example, *take home.take it home, fill up. fill it up.*

This latter example, if expanded, will show more clearly how these sequences are built. There are four "uses" of *fill up* sequences. They are as follows:

(9) (1) fill up
          fill it up (3x)
          fill up

     (2) fill up
          fill [ə] up

     (3) fill up (2x)
          fill it up

     (4) fill up
          fill up [ə]
          fill up it (2x)
          fill up

     (5) fill up

In every case, the short form *fill up* occurs first. When *it* is inserted, apparently it is practiced, for example in (1). The [ə] in (2) indicates that Brenda does not have full control over the insertion of *it.* The [ə] in the final position in (4) followed by two instances of *it* in this position indicates that it took practice to perform this postpositioning of *it.* It is because this postpositioning of *it* comes after eleven instances of *fill up* or *fill it up* that I have considered this form to represent postpositioning. That is, I have considered *fill up* to be basic, *fill it up* secondary, and *fill up it* a development of *fill it up.*

In action and object structures the classification of *it* is somewhat difficult. In some cases, such as the many verb-it constructions, *it* seems to have the status of a full word; in others, if the two-word limit holds, *it* does not have full-word status. This is the reason for suggesting that *it* is an inflectional particle of some kind that represents the place of a longer element that becomes impossible for the child to include in the utterance because of the two-element limit.

There are several good examples of the interaction between the two-word limit and *it*. We have *cut it down* and *tree down* (an apparent exception to the action and object word order, verb-noun). The meaning from the gesture, which was a strong cutting motion, was that Momotaro (Peach Boy) had cut the tree down. A second example *horn off* was said about a picture in which Momotaro had cut the horns off several monsters.

The solution to these apparent exceptions and to the question of the status of *it* can be seen if we consider the underlying form of all the complex verb structures to be verb-noun-verb affix. In the case where the noun appears (as in *tree down*), the verb does not appear. In cases where the noun does not appear, it is optionally zero or represented by *it*, the transitivizing particle.

There is some evidence from one of the other structures to indicate that this is the correct solution. In the group 5 and 6 structures (locative), we see that they may be the same structure, but in combination one or the other of the elements is optional. When the structure occurs by itself, it is a locative noun phrase consisting of preposition-locative, for example, *in dere*. However, in the entity and locative structure either the preposition is not chosen, as in *Brenda here*, or the locative becomes *it*, as in *water on it*.

The cases presented here indicate that there is constraint on the length of horizontal construction. Vertical construction, in constrast, does not appear to be closely constrained. Evidence for the eliminated parts of horizontal constructions can sometimes be found by looking at vertical constructions in which those elements actually appear.

VIII.5   Vertical Construction in the One-Word Period: BRENDA I and BRENDA II

In a BRENDA III vertical construction such as *Brenda.see that.*, it is not difficult to argue that *Brenda* stands in relation of agent to the rest of the construction. The structure of vertical constructions in BRENDA II can be understood in the same way but with some qualifications. First, one of the reasons that *Brenda* can be understood as an agent so easily is the reasonably clear horizontal construction that follows. When horizontal constructions are of one morpheme length, there is no internal structure to refer to in the longer vertical construction. In addition, word class intuitions are much more uncertain. The intuition of a word class is strongly dependent on the adjacent words in a horizontal construction. For example, *picture mark* above is difficult. If it were *red mark* or *dirty mark*, it would be easier to consider *mark* a noun. On the other hand, if it were *pen mark* the intuition that *mark* was a verb would be stronger. In one-word constituent vertical constructions, word classes are more difficult to determine, and the result is that the structure must also be difficult to determine.

With these cautions in mind we can see the following relations in the vertical constructions of Table 17:

(10)   (1) noun—verb: examples E5, E7, E8, E9, E12, E16, and E18. In all of these the semantic relation expressed is agent and action. E18 has an object added with prompting.

(2) verb—noun: E15 and E17. The semantic relation expressed is action and object.

(3) modifier—noun: E10, E21, and E6. The semantic relation is that of entity and attribute. Remember, however, the question raised earlier about the constructional status of these examples.

(4) noun—noun: E2, E3, and E4. These examples all express the possessor and possession relation.

(5) locative—noun: E14. This expresses the entity and locative relation.

It should be noticed that all these except (5) are in the same word order as that found for horizontal construction in (161–162). In (3) there was also one case of the reversed order (noun-modifier). In the case of (2), there were two examples of the reversed order (noun-verb) indicating the same action and object relation.

In the case of words that stand alone—that is, not in vertical construction—I will not make any argument. These words are all listed in Appendix B. There are two words, however, that stand alone and yet clearly indicate semantic relationships: *some* and *share*. *Some* is always used to express a type of dative (benefactive?)

in which Brenda gives something to someone else. *Share* is used in the reverse case when someone else is exhorted by Brenda to give something to her. This is borne out by the fact that as soon as the one-word limit is lifted these constructions occur with the recipient expressed, as in *dog some* of (161).

VIII.5.1   The Three Operations and Basic Semantic Relations in BRENDA II

From the examples given above, it should be clear that many of the basic relations are present in vertical constructions in BRENDA II. Although the word order is not fully regular, there is a high degree of regularity. It is apparent that even as early as BRENDA II the use of word order to express semantic relations is beginning to develop.

There is a fair amount of evidence for Brown's three operations: nomination, recurrence, and nonexistence. The two most common words in the data of BRENDA II are *Brenda* and *Mommy*, and in some of the cases in which they are used they are clearly naming. Of course, there are many other words that are used in the discourse frame of nomination. That is, another speaker asks for nomination by saying, "What's that?" Brenda's word in response can at least tentatively be considered a nomination.

Recurrence is indicated by the frequent use of *more* as well as, perhaps, *my turn*. Brenda often used *my turn* when she was doing something like drawing with a pencil, and Charlotte took it away from her. In this context, *my turn* could mean 'I want to do more drawing' or 'give it back', both of which seem to be indicating some kind of recurrence.

Nonexistence is indicated throughout BRENDA II by the use of *no more* and *hiding*. The continuity with BRENDA III can be seen in the use of *hiding* in both periods.

As far as the eight basic relations are concerned, they are summarized for BRENDA II as follows:

(11) (1) agent and action: strong evidence.
       (2) action and object: good evidence.
       (3) agent and object: no examples.
       (4) action and locative: no examples.
       (5) entity and locative: one example.

(6) possessor and possession: good evidence.
(7) entity and attribute: evidence depends on analysis of these earliest horizontal constructions.
(8) demonstrative and entity: no examples. Also present are the one-word relations:
(9) benefactive: good evidence.
(10) dative: good evidence.

Once again it can be noted that the strongest case can be made for (1) agent and action. I suggested before that there may be something special about the constructions that in adult language are realized as noun phrases. Notice that (7) is the group about which there was some doubt concerning their constructional status. I suggested that they may be simply learned as unanalyzed wholes, for example, *hot water* rather than 'water which is hot'. Whatever the resolution to this problem may be, it is interesting that the semantic relations that are expressed by noun-verb and noun phrase in adult English are among these earliest relations expressed in construction.

VIII.5.2   Evidence from BRENDA I

It becomes rather farfetched to look for these semantic relations as early as BRENDA I. There is evidence, however, for the three operations. It should be remembered that there were words such as ⟨nene⟩ and ⟨dædi⟩ which seemed to function as names. On the other hand, some of the suggested meanings for the most common word, ⟨awəu⟩ indicated recurrence. The mother sometimes thought it meant 'again'. And, finally, in tape (051) Brenda finished drinking a cup of juice, looked into the empty cup and said ⟨nau⟩ twice. The meaning of this is apparently that the juice is gone (i.e., nonexistent).

VIII.6   Interpretation of Vertical Construction

There are two possible interpretations of vertical constructions. The first is that for any utterance there is an underlying form in Brenda's competence that is restricted by some natural performance factors so that in production it must be separated into manageable units. This interpretation would take as proof of longer underlying structures the manifestation in vertical construction of the several elements. The argument is by analogy with the example in phonology of *microphone*, which at one stage was imitated only with difficulty but later, with no additional rehearsal, is pronounced in a fuller form. The implication is that the longer form was always there but not producible by Brenda. Such an approach might find it hard to explain why the fuller form is not always present in vertical construction.

A second interpretation would be the opposite—that there is no deeper form of the utterances that are constructed vertically. This interpretation would claim that the vertical construction is the structure of discourse, and it is only after learning to structure on this broader level that Brenda abstracts from this the ability to make longer constructions within a single utterance.

I think the most plausible interpretation is to assume that both processes are at work to some extent. To accept only the first interpretation would be to forget the important number of times that Brenda does not complete the longer structure without the assistance of interaction with another speaker. To accept only the second ignores the fact that in some cases Brenda moves from one element to the next without outside help. The fact that both of these processes have been observed over a long period of time suggests that the process of the development of syntax is, in fact, an interaction between the internal structures of the child's competence and external structures of discourse.

VIII.7   BRENDA IV (171–172)

When we look at the data of session (171–172), two months later, it becomes obvious that an investigation of constructions of the complexity that are evident in this tape would require much more data. It would warrant a full investigation of the magnitude of BRENDA I and BRENDA II. For this study we have to remain content with this set of notes in the nature of an epilogue to the study that has preceded.

VIII.7.1   Re-emergence of Imitation

One of the most notable phenomena of (171–172) is that of imitation. Since the end of BRENDA II, there was relatively little imitation of any kind. To be sure, there was a high degree of sensitivity to phonetic detail, but nothing of the sort that was found earlier. Then in (171–172) imitation of longer strings emerges for

the first time as an active process. Table 21 gives a good example
of the extent to which Brenda is willing to imitate. When I try
to change the pattern, she says *read it*, which seems to indicate
an attempt to get me back onto the track of imitations.

TABLE 21. Imitations from **BRENDA IV**

Tape	Brenda	Ron
(172)57	fishes	
		Lobster.
58	lobster	
		Shrimp.
59	shrimp	
		Fiddler crab.
60	fiddler crabs	
		This hermit crab.
61	dis hermit crab	
		This is a spider crab.
62	this i pider crab	
63	this is one[a] crab	
		This is a lobster.
64	this i lobster	
		This is a blue crab.
65	dis i a blue crab	
		This is a—shrimp.
66	this is um—spider one	
		Spider one. No, this is the spider crab. Yeah.
67	no	
68	pider crab	
69	dis i yellow fi—	Where's the yellow crab?
70	dis i yellow crab	
		Is that what you said?
71	read it	
		O.K.
72	read it	
		O.K. Let's look some more.
73	dere	

[a] Hawaiian English may have *one* in places where Standard English invariably has *a*.

TABLE 22. Elaboration in BRENDA IV

Tape	Utterance
(172)157	dis goldfish
158	they goldfish
159	this one[a] goldfish
160	I found one goldfish
161	I found one goldfish
162	I—I found one goldfish
163	I found one goldfish
164	I found one fish
165	that one fish

[a] See footnote to Table 21 on the indefinite article in Hawaiian English.

VIII.7.2 A New Type of Repetition

The expected repetitions of longer and longer utterances are found in BRENDA IV, for example, *I like ice cream. I like ice cream.* What is more typical, however, is the repetition with a change of some element, for example, *Charlotte eat it, Charlotte eat mines,* in which the object is changed (note that use of *mines* here is in accord with Hawaiian English). Of the many examples of this type of repetition, which might be better called elaboration, Table 22 gives the most complex example that occurred in order to show to what extent this has developed. Braine (1973, p. 421) has called sequences of this type "replacement sequences." As this example shows, the technique is to keep one element constant while varying the others, apparently a form of play in which the possibilities of systematic construction are explored.

One final example will be given here to demonstrate to what extent Brenda's system has expanded in the two months between (161–162) and (171–172). Brenda says, *Mommy was carrying it. Mommy was carrying it. Mommy was carrying monster book.* From these replacement sequences it is clear that Brenda has developed considerably beyond simple two-word utterances.

VIII.7.3 Construction

Earlier (VII.7.2) I suggested that the limits on construction length might continue lifting. In that case, we would find horizontal constructions of three-word limits with vertical constructions of four-element limits. Of course, this would imply a very complex structure for these constructions. As it turns out, from the evidence of (171–172), Brenda does continue to expand the limits of horizontal constructions, but perhaps these limits are not so clearly established as the scope expands. She also continues to make vertical constructions, but at least in no case on this tape do they consist of more than three elements. There are discourses proper of longer strings, but they are discourses based on interactions with other speakers. Even in some few cases, there appear to be monologues that are somewhat longer than three elements, but they resemble discourses rather than single adult sentences. Obviously, this is only suggestive, and a further study of the development of discourse would have to address itself to these problems.

Here are three examples that indicate three types of vertical constructions.

(13)   (171)12   I like ice cream
          13   I like ice cream
          14   strawberry ice cream

In this case it can be seen that the intent is *I like strawberry ice cream.*

(14)   (172)22   ladybug   (B looking at picture in book)
          23   ladybug
                            (R) Yeah, that's right.
          24   two dems dere

Here the agreement between the pronoun and the *ladybugs* appears to be a case of discourse structuring rather than sentence structuring.

(15)   (171)5   Open it
                            (S) You can open it.
          6   I don't want to

An adult transformational grammar of 6 would probably generate it as /I don't want to open it/ at some underlying level and then delete the complement *open it* optionally. In this case, at least, the optionality of the rule could be eliminated by requiring deletion in the presence of 5, that is, prior statement of the complement.

Whether or not this is the proper description of what Brenda is doing, of course, cannot be determined on the basis of one example. It is interesting to notice, though, her sensitivity to the discourse in this and in other examples we have looked at. It suggests that an analysis of the interaction between sentence and discourse structure at this level of development might be fruitful.

VIII.8 Summary of BRENDA III and BRENDA IV

The discussion of BRENDA III and IV has shown the convergence of several developments that began somewhat independently in BRENDA I. It can be seen now that the development of syntax rather than being an independent phenomenon rests on the foundation of an important earlier integration of phonology, intonation, and discourse. The utterances of BRENDA IV appear to be the result of a long preparatory development, as well as the beginning of what is simply a new and more complex stage of the same development. It should be clear that the discontinuity between the so-called one-word and two-word or three-word stages is the result of focus on only a single aspect of development—the restriction on the length of horizontal constructions. From the point of view of the vertical construction, there is no discontinuity. It can further be seen that vertical construction prepares the system for development.

CHAPTER IX

The Functional Context of Constructions

IX.1 Three Approaches to Function

Many assumptions about function underlie a discussion of structure. The discussions of Chapters 3 through 8, which have focused mainly on the structure of Brenda's utterances, have assumed that these utterances were functional speech as well as instances of structural forms. In some cases the functioning of utterances has been explicitly mentioned. In Chapter 4, I discussed the relationship of intonation to speech act functioning. In Chapter 6, I discussed the interactive functioning of the utterances *hi* and *here* in initiating conversations and controlling topic. In this chapter, these two types of function, speech act function and interactive function, are brought together in a discussion of the whole period of this study—BRENDA I through BRENDA III.

Halliday's work (1973a, 1973b) with his son, Nigel, compares favorably with BRENDA I and BRENDA II. In my discussion of this early period, I will compare my data with Halliday's. In order to get a single framework in which to view speech act functioning to span the entire period BRENDA I through BRENDA III, I will borrow from the work of Searle (1969, n.d.) in spite of some major differences in the use of his terms. Finally, I will discuss some of the more complex vertical constructions, those of BRENDA III, in the larger context of the kind of speech event interaction.

IX.2 Halliday's Functional Approach

Halliday defines six functions during Phase I, 0;9 to 1;6. These functions are: instrumental, regulatory, interactional, personal, heuristic, and imaginative. The instrumental function is glossed as "I want." With these utterances, Nigel indicated that he wanted some goods or objects. The regulatory function Halliday glosses as "Do as I tell you." These utterances are regulatory of the behavior of others. The interactive function is glossed by "me and you" and includes *Hello, yes* (in response to calls) and first name vocatives. "Here I come" is Halliday's gloss for the personal function. These utterances are expressions of feeling, pleasure, or interest. The range of questions that request names of things are included in Halliday's heuristic function, which he glosses as "Tell me why." The imaginative function is glossed as "Let's pretend." A seventh function, informative, emerged at the end of Phase I and beginning of Phase II. This function, which is very characteristic of adult speech, developed late for Nigel (around 1;10).

Halliday claims that the first six of these functions are prerequisite to transition to Phase II. BRENDA I corresponds in age to early Phase I so we might expect to be able to find some evidence bearing on Halliday's claims.

IX.2.1 Phase I

Brenda's most frequent word in BRENDA I is ⟨awəu⟩. The gloss I have used is 'I want'. This, of course, corresponds to Halliday's instrumental function, which he glosses in the same way. Most of Brenda's uses of ⟨awəu⟩ are clearly of this type and, as Halliday suggests, refer to goods or objects. In tape (051) it is used as Brenda tries to pick up ice on two different occasions and in many places as she reaches out to grasp a necklace. This use fits Halliday's instrumental function exactly.

At this same time, however, in one place Brenda says ⟨awəu⟩ when I tickle her, which I took to mean she wanted me to keep doing it. Further, her mother reported that whenever they did something that Brenda liked such as going down the slide Brenda would say ⟨awəu⟩ to get the mother to repeat. This corresponds to Halliday's regulatory function, that is, "Do as I tell you." This function, which controls the behavior of others, is almost as frequent as the instrumental use of ⟨awǝu⟩. Brenda also says ⟨awǝu⟩ while she walks, and her mother encourages her. This may correspond to Halliday's personal function (glossed as 'Here I come').

These few examples indicate that Brenda does have control of at least two of these three functions, but, unlike Halliday's Nigel, Brenda can use a single word for all three functions. To further complicate matters, in many cases Brenda's use of ⟨awǝu⟩ is taken by the mother to be a request for the name of an object. This use fits Halliday's heuristic function.

Halliday's interactive function is demonstrated by Brenda's use of the vocative, *Mommy*, to call her mother and to begin interactions with her. I have no evidence in BRENDA I for the imaginative function, but it is quite well developed at the beginning of BRENDA II, tape (071), which indicates that it has developed some time in the hiatus between the two periods.

Because of major differences in method, it is difficult to establish a very close comparison of Brenda and Halliday's Nigel. Halliday, because he was focusing on function includes a large amount of data from quite varying settings. For each major function group, he is able to show further subdivisions. The data I have for Brenda were collected in a fairly constant setting that in itself precludes a wide variety of function. Halliday's major claim about Phase I is that the six functions are prerequisite to transition to Phase II. This claim appears to be supported even to the limited extent that my data on Brenda are comparable to Halliday's. His secondary claim that there is a one-to-one correspondence between function and form can only be maintained by considering at least the instrumental and regulatory functions to be a single function for Brenda. One quite frequent form, ⟨awǝu⟩, although it is used in the instrumental function as Halliday would expect is also used frequently in the regulatory function, as well as, perhaps, the personal and heuristic functions. It is important to notice that intonation is not used contrastively for these functions (see IV.5 and IX.3.2).

IX.2.2   Phase II

This lack of distinction, particularly between the instrumental and regulatory functions, anticipates Halliday's Phase II. In Phase II, Halliday observed that these two functions merged to form a single function, the pragmatic function. It appears that for Brenda the pragmatic function is undifferentiated much earlier. My data, however, do not allow me to speculate about anything earlier than 1;0.2.

There are several differences which are, perhaps, more crucial between Phase I and Phase II that my analysis of Brenda bears out. First, Halliday claims that the child's Phase I ability is largely taxonomic whereas in Phase II it is systematic. The evidence I have that this is so is just this word ⟨awəu⟩. In BRENDA II the pragmatic function that was served with the single word ⟨awəu⟩ in BRENDA I is served with a progressively widening range of verbs. It is evident that these verbs have replaced ⟨awəu⟩ since ⟨awəu⟩ disappears completely. This taxonomic system can be seen more clearly, however, by using speech act classification as in IX.3.2.

The second difference between Phases I and II is that Phase II is characterized by the simultaneous beginning of both dialogue and grammar. In Chapter 6, I pointed out that dialogue in BRENDA I was virtually nonexistent. What appeared to be dialogue was largely the result of the activity of the adults in interaction with Brenda. By BRENDA II, genuine dialogues were abundant. I also found little evidence of vertical construction before the beginning of BRENDA II. I have argued in Chapters 7 and 8 that vertical construction develops out of dialogues. My observation of the absence of both dialogue and vertical construction in BRENDA I and the presence of both at the beginning of BRENDA II give support to Halliday's claim of this crucial early interaction between function and grammar.

IX.3 The Development of Speech Acts

In order to treat the whole period from BRENDA I to BRENDA III from a single point of view, I have classified Brenda's utterances as speech acts. The work of Austin (1962) and later of Searle (1969; n.d.) has provided me with a general framework for this classification. Although I have used Searle's terminology, the work I have done here differs from his in two important ways. Searle, as Austin before him, has chosen to understand a small group of speech acts in depth. This has meant that in ordinary speech there are many utterances that perform speech acts that have not been given any treatment in the literature. This has been true even in Brenda's speech at this early age.

A second difference is even more important. Speech act

theory as developed by Austin and Searle has used a method of introspection. Speech acts are largely defined by what a speaker intends to do, and, although that intention may fail for a number of reasons, the act is considered the same act. In trying to classify Brenda's utterances as speech acts, I have had no access to Brenda's intentions. In a few cases her persistence or her correction of an adult's interpretation has indicated a consistent intention. In most cases, however, I have had to make inferences based on behavior—Brenda's behavior and her interlocutor's behavior. It is questionable in many cases whether these speech acts defined inferentially on the basis of behavior are the same phenomena as speech acts defined intuitively on the basis of introspection about hypothetical circumstances. The speech acts I refer to are of the former, inferential type and may differ in crucial ways from speech acts as Searle has discussed them. The nature of my data has forced this change of orientation.

IX.3.1 Types of Speech Acts

Table 23 gives twenty types of speech acts that occurred in the data of BRENDA I, BRENDA II, and BRENDA III. They are grouped according to Searle's general classes. The numbering is my own. The table also lists the number of tokens of each speech act for the five tapes (012), (051), (071), (141), and (161–162). A dash (–) indicates that the speech act did not occur during that tape session. This only suggests, of course, that Brenda was not able to perform that act during that period. It may only represent an accidental exclusion.

It is necessary now to clarify these terms. There are two broad classes, utterance acts and illocutionary acts. I do not have any evidence for Searle's third category, perlocutionary acts. Utterance acts are those which do not perform any interactive function in saying them. I have included imitations in this group since the primary function seems to be a noninteractive rehearsal. The displays that occurred followed a long series of requests for display from adults. In saying these utterances, Brenda seems to be trying to avoid interaction. The utterances are always in a soft voice and have a minimal length with no repetition. Finally, the unintelligible utterances have to be classed as utterance acts because they do not succeed in performing any interactive function even though they may well be intended as speech acts.

TABLE 23. Types of Speech Acts

Type	Tape				
	(161–162)	(141)	(071)	(051)	(012)
I. Utterance acts					
a. Imitation	6	19	15	3	2
b. Display	4	11	—	—	—
c. Unintelligible	53	63	Many	Many	Most
II. Illocutionary acts					
a. Representative					
1. Statement, simple, reference	96	47	74	22	2
2. Statement, simple, predication	26	32	26	23	—
3. Statement, complex, reference and predication	45	7	3	—	—
4. Assertion	11	2	—	—	—
5. Statement, fictional	65	46	12	—	—
6. Statement, imaginary	111	—	18	—	—
7. Negative, propositional	—	2	—	—	—
b. Directive					
1. Direct directive	33	47	14	24	4
2. Indirect directive	6	—	—	—	—
3. Self directive	39	38	14	—	—
4. Negative directive	6	1	—	4	—
c. Expressive	2	—	5	—	—
d. Vocative	9	2	—	—	—
e. Commissive	2	1	—	—	—
f. Threat	—	6	—	—	—
g. Handing	2	4	6	—	—
h. Translative	—	3	—	—	—
Total of Types	17	17	10	6	4

The main category of speech acts is illocutionary acts. In performing these speech acts, Brenda does something in saying them. Most of what she does falls under the two main subcategories of representatives and directives. In uttering speech acts classed as representatives, Brenda states, asserts, negates statements or assertions, or in more general terms, she talks about things and their properties. These things may be real (observed in the world around her), fictional (observed in books), or imaginary (entirely made up in imagination). The imaginary statements might also be called metaphoring (Mack 1973) in some cases since what Brenda does is call something by another name intentionally. An example of this is when she stood up in the inverted top of a box and said *bathtub*. Although Searle considers play and fiction "parasitic," I agree with Mack (1973) that these are, in fact, important types of speech acts. These classifications II.a.5 and II.a.6, then, are my own.

The three basic types of statements, simple reference, simple predication, and complex reference and predications need to be clarified further. Searle argues that every act of predication implies an act of reference but that an act of reference does not imply an act of predication. This means that every speech act that is a predication also entails an act of reference. I have only partly followed Searle in this, and as a result I have classed as simple references only those references that stand alone. For example, in (161 and 162) Brenda looks at a group of photographs and names the people in them. This series of proper nouns I have classed as simple references. This use of reference corresponds to Brown's operation of nomination (VIII.2.2).

In classifying simple predications, I have not included the implied reference acts. For example, in tape (071) when Brenda holds up her father's shoe and says, *Daddy*, I have counted this as a simple predication. I have not counted the implied references to 'Daddy' and to 'shoe' as two further simple references. The figures given in Table 23 under II.a.1 and II.a.2 count only the simple references and predications that have surface forms.

The third type of statement, complex statements of reference and predication, are those in which both elements have surface forms. For example, in the horizontal construction *drink soup* both the reference act, *soup*, and the predication act, *drink*, are present. The same kind of speech act is performed in vertical construction through a sequence of utterances. In the vertical construction *finger.touch.*, the reference, *finger*, is present as well as the predication, *touch*. I have considered these two separate utterances to be performing a single speech act, a complex statement of reference and predication.

In other cases, it is not quite so easy to hold to the principle of using only surface forms. In *mama . . . shoe* two reference acts are performed, and the predication is left implicit. I have also called these complex statements because I felt the uttering of the sequence performed a single speech act of predication and reference. As Table 23 shows, these complex statements are performed only as vertical construction becomes active in (071), but finally, in (161 and 162), they may be performed both in vertical and horizontal construction.

Brown's second operation of reference, recurrence, occurred only during a sequence of utterances that I have grouped under II.a.6. Brenda says *more coming out*. There is no way of being sure to what she was referring since all of the objects in this sequence were imaginary. The third of Brown's operations of reference, nonexistence, I have grouped as a complex reference and predication. Brenda makes both vertical (141) and horizontal (161) constructions in which *hiding* (i.e., nonexistence) is predicated of objects or persons that she has named.

I have grouped assertions separately since the illocutionary force is to say with greater strength than a statement that something is true. An example from 161 will illustrate this.

(1) (161)152 cat sleeping

(R) It's a kitten. It's not a cat.

152 dat one cat   (pointing to a different picture)

153 that one cat

The force of Brenda's utterance is intended to show me that I was not looking at the picture Brenda was referring to in her statement of (161)152.

Fictional and imaginary statements are much like the statements of II.a.1 and II.a.2 but for II.a.3 there is an interesting exception. Complex statements did not occur as II.a.6, that is, as imaginary statements, and were abundant as II.a.5, that is, as fictional statements. This point will be taken up in more detail in IX.4. The reason I have not subcategorized these statements into references and predications is that in many cases it is quite difficult to decide whether statements are one or the other when the context is fictional or imaginary. This problem is particularly acute with the imaginary statements where the objects being talked about are entirely in Brenda's mind with the only manifestation being her statements about them. These imaginary statements, II.a.6, correspond with Halliday's imaginative function (IX.2).

The two utterances grouped under II.a.7 were the answer *no* to my two questions *Can you read that, Brenda?* and *Is that what you said?* It seems to be the propositional content of my questions that Brenda is negating in both cases. This is a relatively infrequent type of speech act for Brenda.

Under II.b.1, direct directives, I grouped all of the utterances in which Brenda was directly trying to get someone to do something. These correspond to Halliday's pragmatic function (in Phase II). I have not made subcategorizations for requests for action or requests for information. Indirect directives were rare and consisted of Brenda calling *Mommy* not as a vocative (II.d) alone but with the intent that her mother do something about a situation.

A category not discussed by Searle is self-directives. Self-directives were quite frequent from BRENDA II on. I considered self-directives to be those utterances in which Brenda gave herself imperatives as she carried out some action. This is different from describing her own ongoing behavior, which was a common type of statement. In hearing her make self-directives, one gets the feeling that Brenda needs to say the utterance in order to be able to perform the action. The best and clearest example is the series of utterances in (161) in which Brenda instructs herself in the proper way to treat pictures. These are given as vertical constructions E14, E15, E19, and E21 in Table 20 (VII.7.2). E19 is repeated here to illustrate.

(2) Brenda   (carefully holding photograph flat in
                            both hands)
     this way
     picture mark
     dis is way
     this way (2x)

It is fairly clear from this example and from the mother's report that Brenda has been instructed in the care of photographs. Her self-directive is an internalization of her mother's direct directive. Luria (1959, 1971) argues that this self-directive function is a crucial function of language in developing thought and social behavior.

From Table 23, it can be seen that this function developed for Brenda at the beginning of BRENDA II. This is the same time that dialogue and truly interactive functioning began and suggests that, as Halliday has said, Phase II is the period of transition from a highly personal, nonsocial system to the system of the social, adult language. This self-directive speech may be an important element in the internalization of social function.

The remaining categories need less explanation since they are somewhat rarer. Negative directives are self-explanatory. The expressives of (071) are quite stereotyped. They consist of saying *prettybaby* in a soft, high voice while caressing a doll. Vocatives consist of all summonses. Some of these are proper noun vocatives. Some of these are the handing summonses *here*, *give*, and *some*. The details of summonses are given in VI.4. Commissives are rare. As I have defined them, they are utterances that commit Brenda to further interaction. In most of the cases I observed, Brenda used a summons to commit herself to interaction. Threats, perhaps, need no explanation except that the most frequent, *tape.step*, was also used as a vocative, that is, a summons. I have not considered these threats to be perlocutionary acts as Searle suggests since they were, I think, not genuine threats but pretended threats. Handing has been listed as a separate speech act from vocatives since in some few cases handing occurred with no further commitment to interaction. Finally, there was one instance of a translative speech act. Brenda said, *itai* (Japanese 'hurt' or 'it hurts'). When I said, *what?*, Brenda said, *hurt* three times.

These twenty speech acts are probably the minimum necessary to represent Brenda's speech during this period. Some of them such as II.a.5 and II.a.6, fictional and imaginary statements, or II.b.1, direct directives, could be expanded. It is doubtful that any of these separate categories could be grouped together without misrepresenting what Brenda is able to do with speech during this period. It is important to realize that a single utterance may perform more than a single speech act and that several utterances may perform a single speech act. *Here* is both handing and vocative in some cases. *Tapecorder* is both reference and vocative in one place. Vertical constructions may sequence reference and predication to form a complex statement.

IX.3.2   The Relation Between Form and Function

In my data, only in the earliest data is there a clear correlation between the form of an utterance and its function as a speech act. Table 24 lists the illocutionary acts from (051) cross-classified with the forms that represent them.

Although there is not a perfect correlation between form and function in (051), there is a tendency for nouns (N) to be used for references, ⟨awəu⟩ and *other* to be used for directives, and for *no* and proper nouns (PN) to be used for predications. This taxonomic system suggested above in IX.2.2 where specific utterances perform specific functions is just what Halliday has suggested for Phase I.

In (071) there is still some correlation between form and function as Table 25 indicates.

TABLE 24. Illocutionary Acts of (051)

			⟨awəu⟩	*no*	*PN*	*N*	*other*
II. a.	1.	Reference	—	—	—	22	—
	2.	Predication	—	18	2	3	—
b.	1.	Direct directive	20	—	—	—	4
	4.	Negative	(4, ⟨awəu⟩+*no*)	—	—	—

TABLE 25. Illocutionary Acts of (071)

			Vertical Construction	*Adj*	*PN*	*N*	*V*
II. a.	1.	Reference	—	—	9	65	—
	2.	Predication	—	9	14	3	—
	3.	Reference and Predication	3	—	—	—	—
	5.	Fictional	—	—	8	4	—
	6.	Imaginary	—	—	3	11	4
b.	1.	Direct directive	1	—	—	1	1
	3.	Self directive	—	—	—	8	6
c.		Expressive	2	2	—	1	—
g.		Handing	—	—	3	3	—

In (071) reference is done with nouns as in (051) but also with proper nouns. Proper nouns are used for predication but now also adjectives. Verbs are used mostly for directives, and, as I mentioned above (IX.2.2), they have completely replaced the earlier directive ⟨awəu⟩.

With this background of early development sketched out, we can now turn to the relationship between speech act function and horizontal and vertical construction. The examples above (IX.3.1) in which a single utterance performs several functions and in which several utterances perform a single function are characteristic of late BRENDA II and BRENDA III. This lack of one-to-one correspondence between speech act and utterance form indicates that by the end of BRENDA II Brenda has developed a fairly complex set of relationships between form and function.

To look at this question more closely, I will use the data of (161–162) since that tape was the source of the horizontal constructions of Table 18 and the vertical constructions of Table 20 above (VII.7.1 and VII.7.2, respectively). Table 26 below gives a list of illocutionary acts performed with horizontal constructions in (161–162) grouped by the structural-semantic groups of Table 18.

From the point of view of semantic structure, one can see that a single structure such as agent and action or action and object may perform a wide range of illocutionary acts. In the cases of groups 3, 5, 6, 8, 9, and 10, there are relatively few of these in the sample. It remains an open question whether these semantic structures are limited in the illocutionary acts they may perform because of form-function restrictions or whether these limits are an accident of the data collection.

A second way to look at the same data is to list the illocutionary acts as in Table 27.

From the two tables, 26 and 27, it can be seen that on the whole there is no direct correlation between type and illocutionary act. Imaginary statements may be made in the greatest variety of ways and the action and object construction functions in the performance of the greatest number of illocutionary acts. Even this general statement, however, may be rather insecure for two reasons. In Brenda's imaginary statements, there are no existing referents or other context by which an observer can easily class the utterances as speech acts. The variety, then, may simply be the result of

TABLE 26. Structural-Semantic Groups of (161–162)

1. Agent and action	5. and 6. Entity and locative
II. a. 3. Reference and	II. a. 6. Imaginary statement
predication	b. 1. Direct directive
5. Fictional statement	3. Self directive
6. Imaginary statement	7. Entity and attribute
b. 1. Direct directive	II. a. 3. Reference and
3. Self directive	predication
2. Action and object	5. Fictional statement
II. a. 3. Reference and	6. Imaginary statement
predication	b. 1. Direct directive
4. Assertion	3. Self directive
5. Fictional statement	8. Demonstrative and entity
6. Imaginary statement	II. a. 4. Assertion
b. 1. Direct directive	b. 3. Self directive
3. Self directive	9. Indirect object dative
c. Expressive	II. a. 6. Imaginary statement
3. Agent and object/	10. Idiomatic
Possessor and Possession	II. a. 6. Imaginary statement
II. a. 6. Imaginary statement	b. 4. Negative directive
b. 3. Self directive	
4. Action and locative	
II. a. 2. Predication	
5. Fictional statement	
6. Imaginary statement	
b. 1. Direct directive	
3. Self directive	

TABLE 27. Illocutionary Acts of (161–162)

	Groups
II. a. 2. Predication	4
3. Reference and predication	1, 2, 7
4. Assertion	2, 8
5. Fictional statement	1, 2, 4, 7
6. Imaginary statement	1, 2, 3, 4, 5, 6, 7, 9, 10
b. 1. Direct directive	1, 2, 4, 6, 7
3. Self directive	1, 2, 3, 4, 6, 7, 8
4. Negative directive	10
c. Expressive	2

indeterminacy. On the other hand, action and object structures form the largest single group of horizontal constructions in the data, and the large variety of functions may simply be a result of a larger sample size.

An analysis of vertical constructions shows again this lack of direct correspondence between structural-semantic form and illocutionary function. Table 28 lists the vertical constructions of (161–162) according to illocutionary act.

As this table shows, the majority of vertical constructions are representatives (20 out of 36) or directives (15 out of 36), but that is also true for the data as a whole. It remains an open question whether vertical constructions are frequently used for representatives and directives because there are so many of these speech acts in the data or whether there are so many representatives and directives in the data because the means of expression is so well developed.

A comparison of Tables 27 and 28 shows that horizontal and vertical construction overlap in illocutionary function. They perform the same functions with one exception. Horizontal construction performed a negative directive. There is also some overlap between these two types of construction and the single word utterances of (161–162). Single word speech acts also functioned as predications, assertions, fictional statements, imaginary statements, and in one case a direct directive was performed with a proper noun. Table 29

TABLE 28. Illocutionary Acts Performed by Vertical Constructions in (161–162)

			Number
II. a.	2.	Predication	1
	3.	Reference and predication	8
	4.	Assertion	1
	5.	Fictional statement	9
	6.	Imaginary statement	1
b.	1.	Direct directive	7
	3.	Self directive	8
c.		Expressive	1
Total			36

TABLE 29. Single-Word Illocutionary Acts of (161–162)

			Word
II. a.	1.	Reference	Proper noun, complex noun
b.	2.	Indirect directive	Proper noun
d.		Vocative	*here*, Proper noun
e.		Commissive	*here*, complex noun
g.		Handing	*here*

gives the illocutionary acts performed by single word utterances that were not performed with horizontal constructions or vertical constructions.

The rather negative conclusion of this review of the relationship between structural-semantic form and speech act function is that by BRENDA III there is no clear correlation between form and function. To make any positive conclusion about this relationship one would need much more data of a kind that I do not have available to me for Brenda. One would want data covering a much broader situational and functional range. One would further want comprehension data to add to production data. On the basis of the data I have, I suggest that we look for a form-function correlation elsewhere.

IX.4   Speech Event Structure of (161–162)

The hour of interaction that makes up tape (161–162) is probably best considered part of a single speech event, the tape recording session. This event is characterized by a regular occurrence, a fixed set of participants, a consistent goal, and an overt marker of scene. The details of the setting and participants are given in Chapter 2 and Table 1. The regularity of the participants' expectations is indicated by comments such as the mother's saying when we arrived a little later than usual, "You're later today," or, when we leave, "You'll be here next week?" On one occasion Charlotte said, "When you finish taping Brenda...." and in V.3 I gave an example of Brenda's expectations when she said *tape.tape. word.word.*, and so forth. The goal was, perhaps, one-sided although by BRENDA III even Charlotte was aware that we were trying to record Brenda and did not often try to get central attention during the recordings. The overt marker, of course, was the tape recorder, which everyone knew was running and which was the reference point for the beginning and end of the event as seen by most of the participants.

This event, however, can be further divided into seventeen episodes on the basis of topic change and participant role change. In Table 30 the seventeen episodes of (161–162) are listed with the number of utterances, the number of vertical constructions, and the type of interaction.

These episodes vary considerably in length from episodes 5 and 17, which contain two of Brenda's utterances each, to episodes 15 and 16, which contain eighty-three and eighty-five of Brenda's utterances, respectively. If the episodes are characterized on the basis of the kind of interaction, an interesting correlation between vertical construction and interaction type can be seen.

Episodes 15 and 16 are very nearly the same size in number of

TABLE 30. Speech Episodes of (161–162)

Episode	Number of Utterances	Number of Vertical Constructions	Type
1	17	0	Talking doll
2	9	1	Conversation
3	2	0	R and M conversation
4	65	5	Conversation
5	2	0	R and M conversation
6	10	1	Conversation
7	26	1	Conversation
8	12	0	R and M conversation
9	35	4	Conversation
10	70	5	Conversation
11	20	0	Play, imaginative
12	40	3	Conversation
13	18	1	Conversation
14	17	3	Conversation
15	83	0	Play, imaginative
16	85	12	Book game
17	2	0	Conversation

utterances and yet in 15 there are no vertical constructions and in 16 there are twelve, a third of the total found in this hour. The difference, I suggest, is in the type of interaction. I have described the book game in VI.4.1 as presenting Brenda and the adult to each other in highly fluent interactive roles. In contrast, the imaginative play of episode fifteen is so noninteractive that throughout Charlotte interprets Brenda's utterances to the adults (including the mother) who were watching.

From this point of view the absence of vertical constructions in episodes 1, 3, 5, 8, and 11 may be understood. In episode 1 Brenda and Charlotte are playing with a wind-up talking doll. During the entire time that the doll talks, Brenda's speech is wholly unintelligible. This is the type of unintelligibility I discussed in VI.4.1 and VI.4.2 when Brenda's interlocutor becomes temporarily inaccessible. The same is true in episodes 3, 5, and 8 when I am having a conversation with Brenda's mother. During this time, there are very few utterances at all and no vertical constructions. Episode 11 is of the same type as episode 15. I suggest that the absence of vertical constructions in these episodes is a result of the noninteractive nature of the episode. This tends to reaffirm the general argument of Chapters 7 and 8 that vertical construction is an interactive phenomenon.

It is interesting also to note the type of structures that do occur in this imaginative play session (episode 15). Some of the most varied of the horizontal constructions occurred during this episode. For example, in the *fill up* sequences (VIII.4) both *fill it up* and *fill up it* occurred. If we recall Piaget's distinction between accomodation and assimilation, we can see that the freedom of form showing up in imaginative play demonstrates the assimilation of form to the child's immature structures whereas the complex structuring in the highly interactive book game demonstrates an accomodation of the child's structures to the more complex model of the adult system. This gives general support to my earlier argument that interactive speech is the foundation for the development of adult linguistic structure.

IX.5   Toward a Holistic View of Language Development

In Chapter 2, I began my argument for a holistic approach to the study of Brenda's speech. I argued there that the evidence for vertical construction would not have been preserved if my method had accepted more traditional boundaries such as those between phonology and syntax, syntax and discourse, or structure and function. What I wish to do now that all of the data have been discussed in some detail and from several points of view is to review the ways in which I have observed separate aspects of Brenda's developments to interact.

Beginning with phonology, the phonetic shape of an utterance at any stage of development can be seen to be the result of a complex of factors. The first factor is Brenda's basic phonological ability at the time. For example, in BRENDA I there were no final consonants under any conditions or in BRENDA II all of the clusters of *s* plus another consonant were pronounced as the second consonant alone.

A second factor affecting the phonetic shape of an utterance is the constructional context. The difference between the pronunciation of a word when it occurs in isolation and when it occurs in construction was observed in cases like the examples *mama...shoe*, *tall...clown*, or *finger.touch*. I have suggested that because of the added difficulty of constructing a sequence Brenda used a simpler (earlier) form of the words.

When there is a model for a word immediately preceding Brenda's utterance, she tends to be able to improve her surface form. In (141) Brenda's form [haidi:] 'hiding' changed to [haidiŋ] just after I had pronounced the word for her. Over a series of repetitions, however, her pronunciation drifted back to the more basic form [haidi:]. To study this third factor it is important to have a transcription of the environmental speech since the analysis of Brenda's basic ability depends on comparing only utterances of the same degree of spontaneity.

A fourth factor that may affect the phonetic shape of an utterance is the amount of rehearsal. In the *mama...shoe* example that I have frequently quoted, it took Brenda four attempts at *mama* and seven attempts at *shoe* to say the whole vertical construction. A short time later Brenda said the same thing again as follows:

(3) (071)277 mami ͡ʔ
      278 hyuš
      279 šu
      280 šu

281 šu
282 šu

Notice that this time she switched from the first element to the second after only one token and then within two attempts pronounced an acceptable form of *shoe*. The repetition may have been caused by her interlocutors who were not paying any attention to her. The point I am making is that having rehearsed *mama...shoe* appears to have made it easier to perform the second time. Ideally, then, one would want to have a record of everything the child said to control for this rehearsal factor. Although that is not possible, the simple awareness of the importance of this factor is crucial in making judgements about a child's basic ability on the basis of production data.

A fifth factor came to light in the discussion of Brenda's role taking in interactions. Her role as participant in a speech event and the role of her interlocutors can affect the intelligibility of her speech. When Brenda judges herself to be interacting with someone else and that person temporarily steps out of his interactive role, Brenda's speech becomes unintelligible until that person resumes his interactive role with Brenda. Examples of this occurred when Brenda's mother began speaking Japanese on the telephone, when I spoke a few sentences in an aside to Suzanne, and when Brenda's mother and I carried on a conversation in her presence from which she was excluded because of topic, fluency of our interaction, and our interactive style.

In making a phonological study of a child's speech, then, it is necessary to observe both the speech of the child and the speech of the people with whom she is interacting. It is further necessary to understand the types of interactions and the child's role in them. It is also important to make structural analyses of other types of structuring to be able to set single utterances in their larger constructional contexts.

On another level of structure, the study of horizontal construction is subject to a very similar interplay among factors. There is a basic ability that does not seem to vary significantly under any conditions. I did not find any horizontal constructions in BRENDA I or even in most of BRENDA II. Other observers have been so convinced that horizontal construction represented a basic ability that it is part of the common language to talk of the "two-word period."

Horizontal constructions, however, are also sensitive to the larger constructional context. I observed that there was a restriction on horizontal constructions in vertical constructions so that no strings of the same semantic structure but with different content are possible within a single vertical construction.

Horizontal constructions like single word utterances are affected by the presence of a model. The construction *bump.head.* of (141) was only produced successfully after I had modeled it for Brenda. In (161) the quite complex vertical construction *my turn.do it.* was modeled in part when I said *my turn.* That is to say, because of the model, Brenda did not have to expend constructional effort on the horizontal construction *my turn*, thus allowing her to make the more complex vertical construction.

Rehearsal is also an important factor in horizontal construction. In the set of self directives of (161) where Brenda says *this way* at one time she says *this is way.* This is the only place in BRENDA III where there is any evidence for the copula. This sequence, of course, has been carefully rehearsed. It is also evident, however, that rehearsal is not the only factor involved since Brenda is only able to produce this copula one time. The other times she says *this way* it is a more characteristic horizontal construction without copula.

The place of horizontal constructions in a larger interactional sequence is also important. Horizontal constructions are not used as vocatives or as commissives. These functions appear to be restricted to more routine formal means and do not allow free construction. On the other hand, in events or episodes where there is relatively little structuring of the interaction, such as in Brenda's imaginative play, horizontal construction appears in the widest variety of functions and with the most fluid internal structure. The set of constructions including *fill up*, *fill it up*, and *fill up it* occurred during one of these play sessions.

The study of the syntax of a child's speech, then, is no less complex than the study of the phonology. One must be aware of factors of higher level construction, environmental speech, rehearsal, the interactive role of the child, and the structuring of the speech event.

Vertical construction is basically an interactive phenomenon and can be seen to be most strongly affected by the structuring of the interactive situation. Brenda's ability to make vertical constructions depends crucially on the willingness of her interlocutors to perform their part. This, in turn, depends on the larger speech event structure. I pointed out that in the book game, where roles were clearly defined and interaction was fluent, vertical construction was most abundant. In imaginative play sessions where interaction with adults is most strongly limited vertical construction was also strongly limited.

Because the role structuring of the speech event is so important in vertical construction, Brenda's ability to get and hold the floor is crucial in getting into an interactive role. This, in turn, depends in part on her phonological and constructional development as well as on such other factors as the development of her lexicon and her general knowledge. People are able to interact with Brenda only to the extent that they can understand her. This introduces still another factor. Certain people such as Brenda's mother, because they have a wider experience with Brenda, are able to understand her better. This allows them to take interactive roles with Brenda more easily and because they interact more easily Brenda is able to develop a higher level of performance with them.

What emerges from this review is a picture of the great complexity facing a child learning her first language. Any view that seeks to reduce this complexity for the sake of theoretical ease does an injustice to the child involved in this central and creative human process.

When we try to pick out anything by itself we find it hitched to everything else in the universe.

John Muir

APPENDIX A

Symbols Used

I. General symbols

[ ]	phonetic transcription, e.g., [pʰiŋgə] or [tʰɔč].
/ /	phonemic form, e.g., /nana/ for [nene].
' '	gloss or meaning, e.g., [nene] 'nurture'.

italic   a target word (English or Japanese). This notation is used particularly for the orthographic translation of Brenda's words in BRENDA III and IV. In many cases, it is difficult to maintain a distinction between gloss and target (' ' and *italic*) since the target form and gloss are identical. For example, [šuʔ] (phonetic), *shoe* (target), and 'shoe' (meaning).

" "   quotation, introducing new terms, calling particular attention to a use that is unexpected, unusual, or questionable, e.g., "vertical construction" (a new term) or "pivot-open" (a questionable term).

⟨ ⟩   most general shape of a Brenda word (neither phonetic nor phonemic), e.g., ⟨awəu⟩.

x x x   sounds that, although audible to some extent, could not be transcribed.

    terminal utterance boundary. (See II.3.3 and IX.3 for discussion.) [ ], / /, and ⟨ ⟩ also indicate utterance boundaries.

...		deletion of some number (unspecified) of utterances.
~		variation of the forms on either side, e.g., [s] ~ [š].
(2x)		a number plus x in parentheses represents the number of repetitions, e.g., (2x) indicates two repetitions of the preceding utterance.

utterance boundary is also indicated in the example format by listing separate utterances vertically. When written in the text a period (.) indicates final utterance boundary.

II. Phonetic symbols

Consonants	*bilabial*	*labio-dental*	*dental*	*palato-alveolar*	*palatal*	*velar*	*glottal*
Stop							
Voiceless	p		t			k	ʔ
Voiced	b		d			g	
Nasal	m		n			ŋ	
Liquid							
Nasalized-Lateral			l^n				
Lateral			l				
Rolled			r				
Fricative							
Voiceless		f	ɵ s	š		x	h
Voiced		v	ð z	ž			
Affricate							
Voiceless				č			
Voiced				ǰ			
Semi-Vowel	w				y		

II.   Phonetic symbols—*Continued*

Vowels	Front	Central	Back
High			
tense	i	ɨ	u
lax	ɪ		ʊ
Mid			
tense	e	ə	o
lax	ɛ		ʌ
Low	æ	a	ɔ

Aspiration—raised *h* (occurs in [pʰ], [tʰ], and [kʰ])
Palatalization—raised *y* (occurs in [bʸ], [tʸ], [dʸ], and [kʸ])
Labialization—raised *w* (occurs in [bʷ], [fʷ], and [tʷ])
Syllabic segment— ͺ (occurs in [ļ] and [r̩])
Full length—:
Half length—ˑ
Nasal vowel—˜(e.g., ĩ)
Voiceless vowel— ̥(e.g., i̥)
Primary stress— ′(e.g., báby)

III.   Examples of various notations

(1)	[pʰiŋgə] [tʰəč]	phonetic transcription of a sequence of two utterances as they appear in examples.
(2)	[pʰiŋgə.tʰəč]	the same sequence as (1) as it appears in a line of text.
(3)	*finger* *touch*	target forms (translation) of the utterances of (1) and (2) as they appear in examples.
(4)	*finger.touch.*	the same sequence as it appears in a line of text.
(5)	'I touch it with my finger'	a gloss of the preceding vertical construction.

Words Used in BRENDA II

I. Words Used in More than One Session BRENDA II

baby 071, 081, 131
band-aid 081, 091, 101, 121
bear 071, 091, 101, 111, 121
bed 071, 111
big 071, 131
black 081, 111, 141
blue 071, 111
Brenda 071, 081, 091, 101, 121, 131, 141
broke 091, 131
bucket 111, 131
bug 111, 131
bus 111, 121

car 111, 141
carry 081, 111, 141
cat 101, 131
chameleon 071, 101
Charlotte 081, 091, 101, 111, 141
circle 111, 141
climb 071, 131
cook 081, 101, 141
cookie 071, 121, 131
cow 081, 131
cup 111, 131

daddy 071, 081, 091, 101, 111, 121
dancing 111, 121
down 091, 111, 121, 131

drop 101, 131
duck 081, 091

eat 071, 101, 111, 121, 131
eating 101, 111, 121, 131
egg 101, 111

fall 091, 131
Fang 081, 101
fell 091, 111, 131
finger 121, 141
fish(ing)/(y) 081, 091, 111, 131
flower 091, 101
fly(ing) 101, 131, 141
foot 081, 091

get 091, 111, 121, 131
girl 091, 101, 111
good 111, 121, 141
got 111, 121, 141

hat 071, 081, 091, 111
hiding 101, 141
hole 091, 111
home 101, 121
horsie 071, 081, 091, 101, 111, 121
hot 081, 091, 101, 111, 121
house 101, 131

hurt 081, 141

ice 081, 111, 121

juice 101, 111, 121, 141
jump 071, 101, 131

Kimby 111, 121, 131

lantern 091, 141

mama 071, 081, 101, 111, 131, 141
man 081, 091, 101, 111, 121, 141
milk 101, 141
mine 101, 121, 141
mom 071, 091, 131
mommy 071, 081, 091, 101, 111, 121,
    131, 141
monkey 091, 111, 131
monster 101, 121
more 111, 121, 131
my turn 091, 141

napkin 091, 121
nene 081, 101, 111
nice 071, 081, 091, 101, 111
no 081, 091, 101, 111, 121, 131, 141
no more 101, 111

one 111, 131
open 101, 121
orange 071, 091, 111, 131
otemba 091, 131
own 111, 121

paper 081, 091, 101, 111, 121, 131
pen 071, 081, 091, 111
pencil 071, 081
plenty 081, 101, 111, 131
purple 081, 091, 101

rabbit 101, 121

red 101, 111, 121
Ron 111, 121, 141

see 071, 081, 091
share 101, 111, 141
shishi 081, 101
shoe 071, 101
shoyu 111, 131
sick 071, 081
sit(ting) 081, 091, 101, 111, 121
sleep(ing) 091, 111, 121
slipper 091, 131
soup 101, 131
spill 121, 131
step 101, 131, 141
stuck 101, 111, 121, 141
Suzie 081, 141
swim(ming) 071, 081, 091, 131

take 091, 131
talk 091, 111
tall 091, 121
tape 071, 081, 091, 111, 121, 141
thankyou 081, 121
there 081, 101, 141
tickle 081, 091
toe(s) 081, 121, 141
turn 081, 091, 141
two 081, 111, 121, 131

walk(ing) 071, 101, 111, 121, 141
want (too) 101, 121
water 081, 131
Wendy 081, 091
wet 101, 111
window 091, 141
wowow 071, 081
write 071, 081, 091, 111, 121, 131

yukky 111, 121

Total: 118

II.   Words Used One Session Only BRENDA II

all pau	101	bank	121
ate	121	bark	101
		bash	091
bag	091	bathroom	121
ball	081	Bert	121
balloon	141	birdie	101

blanket	121	face	081
boat	071	fan	111
bone	071	feed	111
book	101	fight	131
boy	141	find	141
brown	081	finish	111
bubble	091	five	131
bump	141	floor	121
burger	081	fork	111
burn	101	four	131
burnt	131	Frankie	121
button	141	fun	111
buyed	121		
		give	141
ca(mera)	141	go	111
cabbage	101	goat	091
can	141	going	141
candy	121	gone	111
catching	111	green	111
cents	111	guava	101
Checkers	071	gum	121
checks	091		
chew	121	hand	071
chicken	131	hankie	071
Cindy	101	head	141
clock	101	heavy	091
close	121	hop	131
clown	091	hot water	131
cold	111	hungry	131
color	081		
come	071	I am	131
cool	111	ice cream	111
'corder	071	in	111
cream	111	it	101
cucumber	101	itai	141
cup cakes	131		
curtain	141	jack-o-lantern	091
cut	071		
		kick	091
dangling	121	kitchen	101
dead	101	kitty	101
deer	131	konbu	101
died	101		
do	111	late	081
dog(gie)	101	leaf	131
Donald	121	lizard	101
doughnut	091	look	091
drink	111	lost	141
		lunch	111
"E"	091		
enough	111	m (and m)	121
Ernie	121	mada	111

make	131	rolling	141
march	111	Ronald	121
me	131	Ronnie	081
men	141	rug	121
microphone	141		
mike	141	said	141
mother	071	sand	131
much	131	sandbox	131
mush	131	scissor	111
		scratches	121
net	071	self	141
nightime	141	seven	131
no fair	131	shell(s)	131
noodle	121	shopping	121
		sit down	081
oh	101	six	131
one more	111	slide	111
oops	141	soft	091
out	131	some	131
ow	091	something	141
owl	141	sour	121
		spoon	111
page	141	swing(ing)	091
paste	091		
pau	081	tamago	101
pay	111	taste	131
pet	111	teddy bear	111
Peter	141	teeth	121
pink	141	ten	131
pink car	141	three	131
pixie	141	thumbkin	121
place	121	tick	101
playing	121	ticket	111
pogo	071	tock	101
pop	141	too	101
pretty baby	071	touch	141
pull	101	trees	131
pumpkin	141	triangle	141
push	111	truck	121
pussy	071	turtle	081
radish	101	waste	121
Raggedy	101	watch	101
rain(ing)	101	went	141
raisin	111	white	101
Ralph	071	wipe	121
rattle	121	witch	141
read	141	wood	131
ready	131	word	111
rice	081		
ride	121	yellow	081
right	111		
rock	101	Total:	201

III.   Most Frequent Words BRENDA II

Frequence (Number of Sessions)	Words	Number of Words
8	Mommy, Brenda	2
7	no	1
6	daddy, horsie, mama, tape, write	6
5	bear, Charlotte, eat, nice, paper, walk	6
4	band-aid, down, fish, get, hat, hot, juice, orange, pen, plenty, sit, stuck, swim, two	14
3	baby, black, carry, cook, cookie, fell, flying, girl, good, got, ice, jump, Kimby, mine, mom, monkey, more, nene, purple, red, Ron, see, share, step, there, toe(s), turn	27
2	(See Table 7)	62
1	(See Table 8)	201
Total for **BRENDA II**		319

Bibliography

AUSTIN, John. 1962. *How to do things with words.* New York: Oxford University Press.

BAR-ADON, A., and W. F. Leopold (eds.). 1971. *Child language: a book of readings.* Englewood Cliffs, New Jersey: Prentice-Hall.

BEVER, Thomas G., Jerry A. Fodor, and William Weksel. 1965. "Theoretical notes on the acquisition of syntax: a critique of 'contextual generalization'." In: Bar-Adon, A., and W. F. Leopold (eds.). 1971. *Child language: a book of readings,* pp. 263–278. Englewood Cliffs, New Jersey: Prentice Hall.

BLOOM, Lois. 1970. *Language development: form and function in emerging grammars.* Cambridge, Mass.: MIT Press.

———. 1972. "Semantic features in language development." In: Schiefelbusch, Richard L. (ed.). *Language of the mentally retarded,* pp. 19–33. Baltimore: University Park Press.

BOWERMAN, Melissa. 1973. *Early syntactic development: a cross-linguistic study with special reference to Finnish.* Cambridge, England: Cambridge University Press.

BRAINE, Martin D. S. 1963. "The ontogeny of English phrase structure: the first phase." In: Bar-Adon, A., and W. F. Leopold (eds.). 1971. *Child language: a book of readings,* pp. 279–289. Englewood Cliffs, New Jersey: Prentice-Hall.

———. 1973. "Three suggestions regarding grammatical analyses of children's language." In: Ferguson, Charles A., and Dan Isaac Slobin (eds.). 1973. *Studies of child language development,* pp. 421–429. New York: Holt, Rinehart and Winston, Inc.

BROWN, Roger, and Ursula Bellugi-Klima. 1964. "Three processes in the child's acquisition of syntax." In: Bar-Adon, A., and W. F. Leopold (eds.). 1971. *Child language: a book of readings*, pp. 307–318. Englewood Cliffs, New Jersey: Prentice Hall.

BROWN, Roger, Courtney Cazden, and Ursula Bellugi-Klima. 1968. "The child's grammar from I to III." In: Bar-Adon, A., and W. F. Leopold (eds.). 1971. *Child language: a book of readings*, pp. 382–412. Englewood Cliffs, New Jersey: Prentice-Hall.

BROWN, Roger. 1973. *A first language: the early stages.* Cambridge, Mass.: Harvard University Press.

BUSH, C. N., M. L. Edwards, J. M. Luckau, C. M. Stoel, M. A. Macken, and J. D. Petersen. 1973. *On specifying a system for transcribing consonants in child language: a working paper with examples from American English and Mexican Spanish.* Child Language Project, Committee on Linguistics, Stanford University.

CHAFE, Wallace L. 1970. *Meaning and the structure of language.* Chicago: The University of Chicago Press.

DALE, Philip S. 1972. *Language development, structure and function.* Hinsdale, Illinois: Dryden Press.

DERWING, Bruce L. 1973. *Transformational grammar as a theory of language acquisition.* Cambridge, England: Cambridge University Press.

DIESING, Paul. 1971. *Patterns of discovery in the social sciences.* Chicago: Aldine-Atherton.

DRACHMAN, Gaberell. 1973. "Studies in the acquisition of Greek as a native language: I. some preliminary findings on phonology." *Working papers in linguistics* 15:99–114. Ohio State University.

EDWARDS, Mary L. 1973. "The acquisition of liquids." *Working papers in linguistics* 15:1–54. Ohio State University.

FILLMORE, Charles J. 1968. "The case for case." In: Bach, Emmon, and Robert T. Harms (eds.). *Universals in linguistic theory*, pp. 1–88. New York: Holt, Rinehart and Winston, Inc.

FRIES, Charles C. 1952. *The structure of English.* New York: Harcourt, Brace and Company.

GRUBER, Jeffrey S. 1967. "Topicalization in child language." In: Bar-Adon, A., and W. F. Leopold (eds.). 1971. *Child language: a book of readings*, pp. 364–382. Englewood Cliffs, New Jersey: Prentice-Hall.

HALLIDAY, M. A. K. 1973a. "Early language learning: a sociolinguistic approach." Paper prepared for the IXth International Congress of Anthropological and Ethnological Sciences, Chicago.

———. 1973b. "Learning how to mean." (In press)

HOCKETT, Charles F. 1967. "Where the tongue slips, there slip I." *To honor Roman Jakobson*, pp. 910–936. The Hague: Mouton.

JAKOBSON, Roman. 1968. *Child language, aphasia, and phonological universals.* The Hague: Mouton.

LABOV, William. 1970. "The study of language in its social context." *Studium Generale* 23:30–87.

———. 1971. "Methodology." In: Dingwall, Wm. Orr. (ed.). *Survey of linguistic science*, pp. 412–497. College Park, Maryland: University of Maryland Linguistics Program.

LEOPOLD, Werner F. 1953. "Patterning in children's language learning." In: Bar-Adon, A., and W. F. Leopold (eds.). 1971. *Child language: a book of readings*, pp. 134–141. Englewood Cliffs, New Jersey: Prentice-Hall.

LEWIS, M. M. 1937. "The beginning of reference to past and future in a child's speech." In: Bar-Adon, A., and W. F. Leopold (eds.). 1971. *Child language: a book of readings*, pp. 64–74. Englewood Cliffs, New Jersey: Prentice-Hall.

LIEBERMAN, Philip. 1967. *Intonation, perception, and language*. Cambridge, Mass.: MIT Press.

LURIA, A. R. 1959. The directive function of speech in development and dissolution. In: Bar-Adon, A., and W. F. Leopold (eds.). 1971. *Child language: a book of readings*, pp. 185–200. Englewood Cliffs, New Jersey: Prentice-Hall.

MACK, Dorothy. 1973. "Metaphoring as one kind of speech act." In: Nilsen, Don L. F. (ed.). 1973. *In honor of Norman C. Stageberg. Meaning: a common ground of linguistics and literature*, pp. 64–74. Cedar Falls, Iowa.

MCNEILL, David. 1966. "Developmental Psycholinguistics." In: Smith, Frank, and George A. Miller (eds.). *The genesis of language: a psycholinguistic approach*, pp. 15–84. Cambridge, Mass.: MIT Press.

———. 1970. *The acquisition of language*. New York: Harper and Row.

MENYUK, Paula, and Nancy Bernholz. 1969. "Prosodic features and children's language productions." *Quarterly progress report*, No. 93, 216–219. MIT Research Laboratory of Electronics. Cambridge, Mass.

MILLER, W. R., and S. M. Ervin. 1964. "The development of grammar in child language." In: Bar-Adon, A., and W. F. Leopold (eds.). 1971. *Child language: a book of readings*, pp. 321–339. Englewood Cliffs, New Jersey: Prentice-Hall.

ODO, Carol. 1973. "Focusing and defocusing in Hawaiian English." In: Bailey, Charles-James N., and Roger W. Shuy (eds.). *New ways of analysing variation in English*, pp. 297–305. Washington, D. C.: Georgetown University Press.

OLMSTED, D. L. 1971. *Out of the mouth of babes: earliest stages in language learning*. The Hague: Mouton.

PAINTER, Colin. 1971. "Archetypal breath group and the motor theory of speech perception: evidence from a register tone language." *Anthropological linguistics* 13(7):349–360.

PIAGET, Jean. 1951. *Play, dreams and imitation in childhood*. New York: Norton.

———. 1969. *The child's conception of the world*. Totowa, New Jersey: Littlefield, Adam and Co.

SARLES, Harvey B. 1972. "Critical naturalism and the new linguistics: back to phonology." In: Smith, Estelle M. (ed.). *Studies in linguistics in honor of George L. Trager*, pp. 66–73. The Hague: Mouton.

SCHEGLOFF, Emanuel A. 1972. "Sequencing in conversational openings." In: Gumperz, John, and Dell Hymes (eds.). 1972. *Directions in sociolinguistics*, pp. 346–380. New York: Holt, Rinehart and Winston, Inc.

SCOLLON, Ronald. 1974. "Language to the crib." Report to the Child Language Project, Social Sciences and Linguistic Institute, University of Hawaii, Ms.

SEARLE, John. 1969. *Speech acts.* Cambridge, England: Cambridge University Press.

——. n.d. "A classification of illocutionary acts." To appear in: *Minnesota studies in philosophy of language.*

SMITH, Nielson V. 1973. *The acquisition of phonology: a case study.* Cambridge, England: Cambridge University Press.

VANDERSLICE, Ralph, and Laura Shun Pierson. 1967. "Prosodic features of Hawaiian English." *The quarterly journal of speech.* 53(2):156–166.

VELTEN, H. V. 1943. "The growth of phonemic and lexical patterns in infant language." In: Bar-Adon, A., and W. F. Leopold (eds.). 1971. *Child language: a book of readings*, pp. 82–91. Englewood Cliffs, New Jersey: Prentice-Hall.